MICROWAVE COOKBOOK 2022

SPEEDY AND DELICIOUS RECIPES FOR BUSY PEOPLE

MEL DEREK

Table of Contents

Fruit and Nut Butter Cheesecake 14
Preserved Ginger Cake 15
Preserved Ginger Cake with Orange 16
Honey Cake with Nuts 17
Gingered Honey Cake 19
Gingered Syrup Cake 20
Traditional Gingerbread 20
Orange Gingerbread 22
Coffee Apricot Torte 22
Rum Pineapple Torte 23
Rich Christmas Cake 24
Fast Simnel Cake 26
Seed Cake 27
Simple Fruit Cake 29
Date and Walnut Cake 30
Carrot Cake 31
Parsnip Cake 32
Pumpkin Cake 33
Scandinavian Cardamom Cake 34
Fruited Tea Bread 36
Victoria Sandwich Cake 37
Walnut Cake 38

Carob Cake	39
Easy Chocolate Cake	39
Almond Cake	39
Victoria Sandwich Gâteau	40
Nursery Tea Sponge Cake	41
Lemon Sponge Cake	42
Orange Sponge Cake	42
Espresso Coffee Cake	43
Orange-iced Espresso Coffee Cake	44
Espresso Coffee Cream Torte	44
Raisin Cup Cakes	45
Coconut Cup Cakes	46
Chocolate Chip Cakes	46
Banana Spice Cake	47
Banana Spice Cake with Pineapple Icing	48
Butter Cream Icing	48
Chocolate Fudge Frosting	49
Fruited Health Wedges	50
Fruited Health Wedges with Apricots	51
Shortbread	51
Extra Crunchy Shortbread	52
Extra Smooth Shortbread	52
Spicy Shortbread	52
Dutch-style Shortbread	52
Cinnamon Balls	53
Golden Brandy Snaps	54
Chocolate Brandy Snaps	55

Bun Scones...56
Raisin Bun Scones...57
Breads 57
Basic White Bread Dough...58
Basic Brown Bread Dough..59
Basic Milk Bread Dough...59
Bap Loaf..60
Bap Rolls 60
Hamburger Buns..61
Fruited Sweet Bap Rolls..61
Cornish Splits 61
Fancy Rolls...62
Rolls with Toppings...62
Caraway Seed Bread..63
Rye Bread 63
Oil Bread...64
Italian Bread...64
Spanish Bread..64
Tikka Masala Bread...65
Fruited Malt Bread 66
Irish Soda Bread...68
Soda Bread with Bran...69
To Freshen Stale Bread..69
Greek Pittas..69
Jellied Cherries in Port..70
Jellied Cherries in Cider..71
Mulled Pineapple...72

Mulled Sharon Fruit 73
Mulled Peaches 73
Pink Pears 74
Christmas Pudding 75
Butter Plum Pudding 76
Plum Pudding with Oil 76
Fruit Soufflé in Glasses 77
Almost Instant Christmas Pudding 78
Ultra-fruity Christmas Pudding 80
Plum Crumble 81
Plum and Apple Crumble 82
Apricot Crumble 82
Berry Fruit Crumble with Almonds 82
Pear and Rhubarb Crumble 82
Nectarine and Blueberry Crumble 83
Apple Betty 84
Nectarine or Peach Betty 84
Middle Eastern Shred Pudding with Nuts 85
Cocktail of Summer Fruits 86
Middle Eastern Date and Banana Compôte 87
Mixed Dried Fruit Salad 88
Stodgy Apple and Blackberry Pudding 89
Lemony Bramble Pudding 90
Lemony Raspberry Pudding 91
Apricot and Walnut Upside-down Pudding 92
Bananas Foster 94
Mississippi Spice Pie 95

Jamaica Pudding *97*
Pumpkin Pie *98*
Oaten Syrup Tart *100*
Coconut Sponge Flan *101*
Easy Bakewell Tart *102*
Crumbly Mincemeat Pie *103*
Bread and Butter Pudding *105*
Lemon Curd Bread and Butter Pudding *106*
Baked Egg Custard *107*
Semolina Pudding *108*
Ground Rice Pudding *108*
Steamed Suet Treacle Pudding *109*
Marmalade or Honey Pudding *109*
Ginger Pudding *110*
Jam Sponge Pudding *110*
Lemon Sponge Pudding *111*
Crêpes Suzette *112*
Baked Apples *113*
Braised Beef and Vegetables *114*
Beef Stew *115*
Beef and Vegetable Hot-pot *116*
Beef Curry *117*
Basic Mince *118*
Cottage Pie *119*
Cottage Pie with Cheese *119*
Mince with Oats *120*
Chilli con Carne *120*

Curried Mince *121*
Beef Goulash *122*
Beef Goulash with Boiled Potatoes *123*
Butter Bean and Beef Stew with Tomatoes *123*
Beef and Tomato Cake *124*
Beef and Mushroom Kebabs *125*
Stuffed Lamb *127*
Minted Lamb Kebabs *128*
Classic Lamb Kebabs *129*
Middle Eastern Lamb with Fruit *130*
Mock Irish Stew *131*
Farmer's Wife Lamb Chops *132*
Lamb Hot-pot *133*
Lamb Loaf with Mint and Rosemary *134*
Lamb Bredie with Tomatoes *135*
Lamb Biriani *136*
Ornate Biriani *137*
Moussaka *138*
Moussaka with Potatoes *139*
Quick Moussaka *140*
Lamb Mince *141*
Shepherd's Pie *141*
Country Liver in Red Wine *142*
Liver and Bacon *143*
Liver and Bacon with Apple *144*
Kidneys in Red Wine with Brandy *145*
Venison Steaks with Oyster Mushrooms and Blue Cheese *147*

Cooking Small Pasta 148
Chinese Noodle and Mushroom Salad with Walnuts 148
Pepper Macaroni 149
Family Macaroni Cheese 150
Classic Macaroni Cheese 151
Macaroni Cheese with Stilton 152
Macaroni Cheese with Bacon 152
Macaroni Cheese with Tomatoes 152
Spaghetti Carbonara 153
Pizza-style Macaroni Cheese 154
Spaghetti Cream with Spring Onions 155
Spaghetti Bolognese 156
Spaghetti with Turkey Bolognese Sauce 157
Spaghetti with Ragu Sauce 158
Spaghetti with Butter 159
Pasta with Garlic 160
Spaghetti with Beef and Mixed Vegetable Bolognese Sauce 161
Spaghetti with Meat Sauce and Cream 162
Spaghetti with Marsala Meat Sauce 162
Pasta alla Marinara 163
Pasta Matriciana 164
Pasta with Tuna and Capers 165
Pasta Napoletana 166
Pasta Pizzaiola 167
Pasta with Peas 167
Pasta with Chicken Liver Sauce 167
Pasta with Anchovies 168

Ravioli with Sauce *168*
Tortellini *169*
Lasagne *170*
Pizza Napoletana *171*
Pizza Margherita *172*
Seafood Pizza *172*
Pizza Siciliana *172*
Mushroom Pizza *172*
Ham and Pineapple Pizza *173*
Pepperoni Pizzas *173*
Buttered Flaked Almonds *174*
Flaked Almonds in Garlic Butter *174*
Dried Chestnuts *174*
Drying Herbs *175*
Crisping Breadcrumbs *176*
Nut Burgers *177*
Nutkin Cake *178*
Buckwheat *179*
Bulgar *180*
Bulgar with Fried Onion *181*
Tabbouleh *182*
Sultan's Salad *183*
Couscous *184*
Grits *185*
Gnocchi alla Romana *186*
Ham Gnocchi *187*
Millet *188*

Polenta	189
Grilled Polenta	190
Polenta with Pesto	190
Polenta with Sun-dried Tomato or Olive Paste	190
Quinoa	191
Romanian Polenta	192
Curried Rice	193
Cottage Cheese and Rice Casserole	194
Italian Risotto	195
Mushroom Risotto	196
Brazilian Rice	196
Spanish Rice	197
Plain Turkish Pilaf	198
Rich Turkish Pilaf	199
Thai Rice with Lemon Grass, Lime Leaves and Coconut	200
Okra with Cabbage	201
Red Cabbage with Apple	202
Red Cabbage with Wine	204
Norwegian Sour Cabbage	204
Greek-style Stewed Okra with Tomatoes	205
Greens with Tomatoes, Onions and Peanut Butter	206
Sweet-sour Creamed Beetroot	207
Beetroot in Orange	208
Scalloped Celeriac	209
Celeriac with Orange Hollandaise Sauce	210
Slimmers' Vegetable Pot	211
Slimmers' Vegetable Pot with Eggs	211

Ratatouille *212*
Caramelised Parsnips *213*
Parsnips with Egg and Butter Crumb Sauce *214*
Fonduta *215*
Mock Cheese and Tomato Fondue *215*
Mock Cheese and Celery Fondue *216*
Italian Cheese, Cream and Egg Fondue *217*
Dutch Farmhouse Fondue *218*
Farmhouse Fondue with a Kick *219*

Fruit and Nut Butter Cheesecake

Serves 8–10

A continental-style cheesecake, the sort you'd find in a quality patisserie.

45 ml/3 tbsp flaked (slivered) almonds
75 g/3 oz/2/3 cup butter
175 g/6 oz/1½ cups oaten biscuit (cookie) or digestive biscuit (Graham cracker) crumbs
450 g/1 lb/2 cups curd (smooth cottage) cheese, at kitchen temperature
125 g/4 oz/½ cup caster (superfine) sugar
15 ml/1 tbsp cornflour (cornstarch)
3 eggs, at kitchen temperature, beaten
Juice of ½ fresh lime or lemon
30 ml/2 tbsp raisins

Put the almonds on a plate and toast, uncovered, on Full for 2–3 minutes. Melt the butter, uncovered, on Defrost for 2–2½ minutes. Thoroughly butter a 20 cm/8 in diameter dish and cover the base and side with the biscuit crumbs. Beat the cheese with all the remaining ingredients and stir in the almonds and melted butter. Spread evenly over the biscuit crumbs and cover loosely with kitchen paper. Cook on Defrost for 24 minutes, turning the dish four times. Remove from the microwave and leave to cool. Chill for at least 6 hours before cutting.

Preserved Ginger Cake

Serves 8

225 g/8 oz/2 cups self-raising (self-rising) flour
10 ml/2 tsp mixed (apple-pie) spice
125 g/4 oz/½ cup butter or margarine, at kitchen temperature
125 g/4 oz/½ cup light soft brown sugar
100 g/4 oz/1 cup chopped preserved ginger in syrup
2 eggs, beaten
75 ml/5 tbsp cold milk
Icing (confectioners') sugar, for dusting

Closely line a 20 cm/8 in diameter soufflé or similar straight-sided dish with clingfilm (plastic wrap), allowing it to hang very slightly over the edge. Sift the flour and spice into a bowl. Finely rub in the butter or margarine. Fork in the sugar and ginger, making sure they are evenly distributed. Stir to a soft consistency with the eggs and milk. When smoothly combined, spoon into the prepared dish and cover lightly with kitchen paper. Cook on Full for 6½–7½ minutes until the cake is well risen and beginning to shrink away from the side. Allow to stand for 15 minutes. Transfer to a wire rack by holding the clingfilm. Peel away the wrap when cold and store the cake in an airtight container. Dust with icing sugar before serving.

Preserved Ginger Cake with Orange

Serves 8

Prepare as for Preserved Ginger Cake, but add the coarsely grated peel of 1 small orange with the eggs and milk.

Honey Cake with Nuts

Serves 8–10

A star of a cake, full of sweetness and light. It is Greek in origin, where it is known as karithopitta. Serve it with coffee at the end of a meal.

For the base:
100 g/3½ oz/½ cup butter, at kitchen temperature
175 g/6 oz/¾ cup light soft brown sugar
4 eggs, at kitchen temperature
5 ml/1 tsp vanilla essence (extract)
10 ml/2 tsp bicarbonate of soda (baking soda)
10 ml/2 tsp baking powder
5 ml/1 tsp ground cinnamon
75 g/3 oz/¾ cup plain (all-purpose) flour
75 g/3 oz/¾ cup cornflour (cornstarch)
100 g/3½ oz/1 cup flaked (slivered) almonds

For the syrup:
200 ml/7 fl oz/scant 1 cup warm water
60 ml/4 tbsp dark soft brown sugar
5 cm/2 in piece cinnamon stick
5 ml/1 tsp lemon juice
150 g/5 oz/2/3 cup clear dark honey

For decoration:

60 ml/4 tbsp chopped mixed nuts
30 ml/2 tbsp clear dark honey

To make the base, closely line the base and side of an 18 cm/7 in diameter soufflé dish with clingfilm (plastic wrap), allowing it to hang very slightly over the edge. Put all the ingredients except the almonds in a food processor bowl and run the machine until smooth and evenly combined. Pulse in the almonds briefly to stop them breaking up too much. Spread the mixture into the prepared dish and cover lightly with kitchen paper. Cook on Full for 8 minutes, turning the dish twice, until the cake has risen appreciably and the top is peppered with small air pockets. Allow to stand for 5 minutes, then invert into a shallow serving dish and peel away the clingfilm.

To make the syrup, place all the ingredients in a jug and cook, uncovered, on Full for 5–6 minutes or until the mixture just begins to bubble. Watch closely in case it starts to boil over. Allow to stand for 2 minutes, then gently stir round with a wooden spoon to mix the ingredients smoothly. Spoon slowly over the cake until all the liquid is absorbed. Combine the nuts and honey in small dish. Warm through, uncovered, on Full for 1½ minutes. Spread or spoon over the top of the cake.

Gingered Honey Cake

Serves 10–12

45 ml/3 tbsp orange marmalade
225 g/8 oz/1 cup clear dark honey
2 eggs
125 ml/4 fl oz/½ cup corn or sunflower oil
150 ml/¼ pt/2/3 cup warm water
250 g/9 oz/generous 2 cups self-raising (self-rising) flour
5 ml/1 tsp bicarbonate of soda (baking soda)
3 tsp ground ginger
10 ml/2 tsp ground allspice
5 ml/1 tsp ground cinnamon

Closely line a deep 1.75 litre/3 pt/7½ cup soufflé dish with clingfilm (plastic wrap), allowing it to hang very slightly over the edge. Put the marmalade, honey, eggs, oil and water in a food processor and blend until smooth, then switch off. Sift together all the remaining ingredients and spoon into the processor bowl. Run the machine until the mixture is well combined. Spoon into the prepared dish and cover lightly with kitchen paper. Cook on Full for 10–10½ minutes until the cake is well risen and the top is covered with tiny air holes. Allow to cool almost completely in the dish, then transfer to a wire rack by holding the clingfilm. Carefully peel away the clingfilm and leave until completely cold. Store in an airtight container for 1 day before cutting.

Gingered Syrup Cake

Serves 10–12

Prepare as for Gingered Honey Cake, but substitute golden (light corn) syrup for the honey.

Traditional Gingerbread

Serves 8–10

A winter's tale of the best kind, essential for Hallowe'en and Guy Fawkes night.

175 g/6 oz/1½ cups plain (all-purpose) flour
15 ml/1 tbsp ground ginger
5 ml/1 tsp ground allspice
10 ml/2 tsp bicarbonate of soda (baking soda)
125 g/4 oz/1/3 cup golden (light corn) syrup
25 ml/1½ tbsp black treacle (molasses)
30 ml/2 tbsp dark soft brown sugar
45 ml/3 tbsp lard or white cooking fat (shortening)
1 large egg, beaten
60 ml/4 tbsp cold milk

Closely line the base and side of a 15 cm/6 in diameter soufflé dish with clingfilm (plastic wrap), allowing it to hang very slightly over the edge. Sift the flour, ginger, allspice and bicarbonate of soda into a mixing bowl. Put the syrup, treacle, sugar and fat in another bowl and heat, uncovered, on Full for 2½–3 minutes until the fat has just melted.

Stir well to blend. Mix with a fork into the dry ingredients with the egg and milk. When well combined, transfer to the prepared dish and cover lightly with kitchen paper. Cook on Full for 3–4 minutes until the gingerbread is well risen with a hint of a shine across the top. Allow to stand 10 minutes. Transfer to a wire rack by holding the clingfilm. Peel away the clingfilm and store the gingerbread in an airtight container for 1–2 days before cutting.

Orange Gingerbread

Serves 8–10

Prepare as for Traditional Gingerbread, but add the finely grated peel of 1 small orange with the egg and milk.

Coffee Apricot Torte

Serves 8

4 digestive biscuits (Graham crackers), finely crushed
225 g/8 oz/1 cup butter or margarine, at kitchen temperature
225 g/8 oz/1 cup dark soft brown sugar
4 eggs, at kitchen temperature
225 g/8 oz/2 cups self-raising (self-rising) flour
75 ml/5 tbsp coffee and chicory essence (extract)
425 g/14 oz/1 large can apricot halves, drained
300 ml/½ pt/1¼ cups double (heavy) cream
90 ml/6 tbsp flaked (slivered) almonds, toasted

Brush two shallow 20 cm/8 inch diameter dishes with melted butter, then line the bases and sides with the biscuit crumbs. Cream together the butter or margarine and sugar until light and fluffy. Beat in the eggs one at a time, adding 15 ml/1 tbsp flour with each. Fold in the remaining flour alternately with 45 ml/3 tbsp of the coffee essence. Spread equally into the prepared dishes and cover loosely with kitchen paper. Cook, one at a time, on Full for 5 minutes. Allow to cool in the dishes for 5 minutes, then invert on to a wire rack. Chop three of the apricots and set aside the remainder. Whip the cream with the remaining coffee essence until thick. Take out about a quarter of the cream and stir in the chopped apricots. Use to sandwich the cakes together. Cover the top and sides with the remaining cream. Press the almonds against the side and decorate the top with the reserved apricots, cut sides down.

Rum Pineapple Torte

Serves 8

Prepare as for Coffee Apricot Torte, but omit the apricots. Flavour the cream with 30 ml/2 tbsp dark rum instead of the coffee essence (extract). Stir 2 chopped canned pineapple rings into three-quarters of the cream and use to sandwich the cakes together. Cover the top and sides with the remaining cream and decorate with halved pineapple rings. Stud with green and yellow glacé (candied) cherries, if wished.

Rich Christmas Cake

Makes 1 large family cake

A luxurious cake, full of the splendours of Christmas and well endowed with alcohol. Keep it plain or coat it with marzipan (almond paste) and white icing (frosting).

200 ml/7 fl oz/scant 1 cup sweet sherry
75 ml/5 tbsp brandy
5 ml/1 tsp mixed (apple-pie) spice
5 ml/1 tsp vanilla essence (extract)
10 ml/2 tsp dark soft brown sugar
350 g/12 oz/2 cups mixed dried fruit (fruit cake mix)
15 ml/1 tbsp chopped mixed peel
15 ml/1 tbsp red glacé (candied) cherries
50 g/2 oz/1/3 cup dried apricots
50 g/2 oz/1/3 cup chopped dates
Finely grated peel of 1 small orange
50 g/2 oz/½ cup chopped walnuts
125 g/4 oz/½ cup unsalted (sweet) butter, melted
175 g/6 oz/¾ cup dark soft brown sugar
125 g/4 oz/1 cup self-raising (self-rising) flour
3 small eggs

Put the sherry and brandy in a large mixing bowl. Cover with a plate and cook on Full for 3–4 minutes until the mixture just begins to bubble. Add the spice, vanilla, the 10 ml/2 tsp brown sugar, the dried fruit, mixed peel, cherries, apricots, dates, orange peel and walnuts. Mix thoroughly. Cover with a plate and warm through on Defrost for 15 minutes, stirring four times. Leave overnight for the flavours to mature. Closely line a 20 cm/8 in diameter soufflé dish with clingfilm (plastic wrap), allowing it to hang very slightly over the edge. Stir the butter, brown sugar, flour and eggs into the cake mixture. Spoon into the prepared dish and cover loosely with kitchen paper. Cook on Defrost for 30 minutes, turning four times. Allow to stand in the microwave for 10 minutes. Cool to lukewarm, then carefully transfer to a wire rack by holding the clingfilm. Peel away the clingfilm when the cake is cold. To store, wrap in a double thickness of greaseproof (waxed) paper, then wrap again in foil. Store in a cool place for about 2 weeks before covering and icing.

Fast Simnel Cake

Makes 1 large family cake

Follow the recipe for Rich Christmas Cake and store for 2 weeks. The day before serving, cut the cake in half to make two layers. Brush both cut sides with melted apricot jam (conserve) and sandwich together with 225–300 g/8–11 oz marzipan (almond paste) rolled out to a thick round. Decorate the top with shop-bought miniature Easter eggs and chicks.

Seed Cake

Serves 8

A reminder of old times, known in Wales as shearing cake.

225 g/8 oz/2 cups self-raising (self-rising) flour
125 g/4 oz/½ cup butter or margarine
175 g/6 oz/¾ cup light soft brown sugar
Finely grated peel of 1 lemon
10–20 ml/2–4 tsp caraway seeds
10 ml/2 tsp grated nutmeg
2 eggs, beaten
150 ml/¼ pt/2/3 cup cold milk
75 ml/5 tbsp icing (confectioners') sugar, sifted
10–15 ml/2–3 tsp lemon juice

Closely line the base and side of a 20 cm/8 in diameter soufflé dish with clingfilm (plastic wrap), allowing it to hang very slightly over the edge. Sift the flour into a bowl and rub in the butter or margarine. Add the brown sugar, lemon peel, caraway seeds and nutmeg and mix in the eggs and milk with a fork to form a smooth, fairly soft batter. Transfer to the prepared dish and cover loosely with kitchen paper. Cook on Full for 7–8 minutes, turning the dish twice until the cake has risen to the top of the dish and the surface is peppered with small holes. Allow to stand for 6 minutes, then invert on to a wire rack. When completely cold, peel away the clingfilm, then turn the cake the right way up. Combine the icing sugar and lemon juice to make a thickish paste. Spread over the top of the cake.

Simple Fruit Cake

Serves 8

225 g/8 oz/2 cups self-raising (self-rising) flour
10 ml/2 tsp mixed (apple-pie) spice
125 g/4 oz/½ cup butter or margarine
125 g/4 oz/½ cup light soft brown sugar
175 g/6 oz/1 cup mixed dried fruit (fruit cake mix)
2 eggs
75 ml/5 tbsp cold milk
75 ml/5 tbsp icing (confectioners') sugar

Closely line an 18 cm/7 in diameter soufflé dish with clingfilm (plastic wrap), allowing it to hang very slightly over the edge. Sift the flour and spice into a bowl and rub in the butter or margarine. Add the sugar and dried fruit. Beat together the eggs and milk and pour into the dry ingredients, stirring to a smooth soft consistency with a fork. Spoon into the prepared dish and cover loosely with kitchen paper. Cook on Full for 6½–7 minutes until the cake is well risen and just beginning to shrink away from the side of the dish. Remove from the microwave and allow to stand for 10 minutes. Transfer to a wire rack by holding the clingfilm. When completely cold, peel away the clingfilm and dust the top with sifted icing sugar.

Date and Walnut Cake

Serves 8

Prepare as for Simple Fruit Cake, but substitute a mixture of chopped dates and walnuts for the dried fruit.

Carrot Cake

Serves 8

Once called paradise cake, this transatlantic import has been with us for a good many years and never loses its appeal.

For the cake:
3–4 carrots, cut into chunks
50 g/2 oz/½ cup walnut pieces
50 g/2 oz/½ cup packeted chopped dates, rolled in sugar
175 g/6 oz/¾ cup light soft brown sugar
2 large eggs, at kitchen temperature
175 ml/6 fl oz/¾ cup sunflower oil
5 ml/1 tsp vanilla essence (extract)
30 ml/2 tbsp cold milk
150 g/5 oz/1¼ cups plain (all-purpose) flour
5 ml/1 tsp baking powder
4 ml/¾ tsp bicarbonate of soda (baking soda)
5 ml/1 tsp mixed (apple-pie) spice

For the cream cheese frosting:
175 g/6 oz/¾ cup full-fat cream cheese, at kitchen temperature
5 ml/1 tsp vanilla essence (extract)
75 g/3 oz/½ cup icing (confectioners') sugar, sifted
15 ml/1 tbsp freshly squeezed lemon juice

To make the cake, brush a 20 cm/8 in diameter microwave ring mould with oil and line the base with non-stick parchment paper. Put the carrots and walnut pieces into a blender or food processor and run the machine until both are coarsely chopped. Transfer to a bowl and work in the dates, sugar, eggs, oil, vanilla essence and milk. Sift together the dry ingredients, then stir into the carrot mixture with a fork. Transfer to the prepared mould. Cover with clingfilm (plastic wrap) and slit it twice to allow steam to escape. Cook on Full for 6 minutes, turning three times. Allow to stand for 15 minutes, then turn out on to a wire rack. Remove the paper. Invert on to a plate when cooled completely.

To make the cream cheese frosting, beat the cheese until smooth. Add the rest of the ingredients and beat lightly until smooth. Spread thickly over the top of the cake.

Parsnip Cake

Serves 8

Prepare as for Carrot Cake, but substitute 3 small parsnips for the carrots.

Pumpkin Cake

Serves 8

Prepare as for Carrot Cake, but substitute peeled pumpkin for the carrots, allowing a medium wedge which should yield about 175 g/6 oz seeded flesh. Substitute dark soft brown sugar for light and allspice for the mixed (apple-pie) spice.

Scandinavian Cardamom Cake

Serves 8

Cardamom is much used in Scandinavian baking and this cake is a typical example of northern hemisphere exotica. Try your local ethnic food shop if you have any trouble getting the ground cardamom.

For the cake:
175 g/6 oz/1½ cups self-raising (self-rising) flour
2.5 ml/½ tsp baking powder
75 g/3 oz/2/3 cup butter or margarine, at kitchen temperature
75 g/3 oz/2/3 cup light soft brown sugar
10 ml/2 tsp ground cardamom
1 egg
Cold milk

For the topping:
30 ml/2 tbsp flaked (slivered) almonds, toasted
30 ml/2 tbsp light soft brown sugar
5 ml/1 tsp ground cinnamon

Line a deep 16.5 cm/6½ in diameter dish with clingfilm (plastic wrap), allowing it to hang very slightly over the edge. Sift the flour and baking powder into a bowl and rub in the butter or margarine finely. Add the sugar and cardamom. Beat the egg in a measuring jug and make up to 150 ml/¼ pt/2/3 cup with milk. Stir into the dry ingredients with a fork until well mixed but avoid beating. Pour into the prepared dish. Combine the topping ingredients and sprinkle over the cake. Cover with clingfilm and slit it twice to allow steam to escape. Cook on Full for 4 minutes, turning twice. Allow to stand for 10 minutes, then carefully transfer to a wire rack by holding the clingfilm. Carefully peel away the clingfilm when the cake is cold.

Fruited Tea Bread

Makes 8 slices

225 g/8 oz/1 1/3 cups mixed dried fruit (fruit cake mix)
100 g/3½ oz/½ cup dark soft brown sugar
30 ml/2 tbsp cold strong black tea
100 g/4 oz/1 cup self-raising (self-rising) wholemeal flour
5 ml/1 tsp ground allspice
1 egg, at kitchen temperature, beaten
8 whole almonds, blanched
30 ml/2 tbsp golden (light corn) syrup
Butter, for spreading

Closely line the base and side of a 15 cm/6 in diameter soufflé dish with clingfilm (plastic wrap), allowing it to hang very slightly over the side. Put the fruit, sugar and tea into a bowl, cover with a plate and cook on Full for 5 minutes. Stir in the flour, allspice and egg with a fork, then transfer to the prepared dish. Arrange the almonds on top. Cover loosely with kitchen paper and cook on Defrost for 8–9 minutes until the cake is well risen and beginning to shrink away from the side of the dish. Allow to stand for 10 minutes, then transfer to a wire rack by holding the clingfilm. Warm the syrup in a cup on Defrost for 1½ minutes. Peel the clingfilm off the cake and brush the top with the warmed syrup. Serve sliced and buttered.

Victoria Sandwich Cake

Serves 8

175 g/6 oz/1½ cups self-raising (self-rising) flour
175 g/6 oz/¾ cup butter or margarine, at kitchen temperature
175 g/6 oz/¾ cup caster (superfine) sugar
3 eggs, at kitchen temperature
45 ml/3 tbsp cold milk
45 ml/3 tbsp jam (conserve)
120 ml/4 fl oz/½ cup double (heavy) or whipping cream, whipped
Icing (confectioners') sugar, sifted, for dusting

Line the bases and sides of two shallow 20 cm/8 in diameter dishes with clingfilm (plastic wrap), allowing it to hang very slightly over the edge. Sift the flour on to a plate. Cream together the butter or margarine and sugar until the mixture is light and fluffy and the consistency of whipped cream. Beat in the eggs one at a time, adding 15 ml/1 tbsp flour with each. Fold in the remaining flour alternately with the milk using a large metal spoon. Spread equally into the prepared dishes. Cover loosely with kitchen paper. Cook one at a time on Full for 4 minutes. Allow to cool to lukewarm, then invert on to a wire rack. Peel away the clingfilm and leave until completely cold. Sandwich together with the jam and whipped cream and dust the top with icing sugar before serving.

Walnut Cake

Serves 8

175 g/6 oz/1½ cups self-raising (self-rising) flour
175 g/6 oz/¾ cup butter or margarine, at kitchen temperature
5 ml/1 tsp vanilla essence (extract)
175 g/6 oz/¾ cup caster (superfine) sugar
3 eggs, at kitchen temperature
50 g/2 oz/½ cup walnuts, finely chopped
45 ml/3 tbsp cold milk
2 quantities Butter Cream Icing
16 walnut halves, to decorate

Line the bases and sides of two shallow 20 cm/8 in diameter dishes with clingfilm (plastic wrap), allowing it to hang very slightly over the edge. Sift the flour on to a plate. Cream together the butter or margarine, vanilla essence and sugar until the mixture is light and fluffy and the consistency of whipped cream. Beat in the eggs one at a time, adding 15 ml/1 tbsp flour with each. Using a large metal spoon, fold in the walnuts with the remaining flour alternately with the milk. Spread equally into the prepared dishes. Cover loosely with kitchen paper. Cook one at a time on Full for 4½ minutes. Allow to cool to lukewarm, then invert on to a wire rack. Peel away the clingfilm and leave until completely cold. Sandwich together with half the icing (frosting) and top the cake with the remainder. Arrange a border of walnut halves on the top of the cake to decorate.

Carob Cake

Serves 8

Prepare as for Victoria Sandwich Cake but substitute 25 g/1 oz/¼ cup cornflour (cornstarch) and 25 g/1 oz/¼ cup carob powder for 50 g/2 oz/½ cup of the flour. Sandwich together with cream and/or canned or fresh fruit. Add 5 ml/1 tsp vanilla essence (extract) to the creamed ingredients, if wished.

Easy Chocolate Cake

Serves 8

Prepare as for Victoria Sandwich Cake, but substitute 25 g/1 oz/¼ cup cornflour (cornstarch) and 25 g/1 oz/¼ cup cocoa (unsweetened chocolate) powder for 50 g/2 oz/½ cup of the flour. Sandwich together with cream and/or chocolate spread.

Almond Cake

Serves 8

Prepare as for Victoria Sandwich Cake, but substitute 40 g/1½ oz/3 tbsp ground almonds for the same amount of flour. Flavour the creamed ingredients with 2.5–5 ml/½–1 tsp almond essence (extract). Sandwich together with smooth apricot jam (conserve) and a thin round of marzipan (almond paste).

Victoria Sandwich Gâteau

Serves 8

Prepare as for Victoria Sandwich Cake or any of the variations. Sandwich together with cream or Butter Cream Icing (frosting) and/or jam (conserve), chocolate spread, peanut butter, orange or lemon curd, orange marmalade, canned fruit filling, honey or marzipan (almond paste). Coat the top and side with cream or Butter Cream Icing. Decorate with fresh or preserved fruits, nuts or dragees. For an even richer cake, halve each baked layer to make total of four layers before filling.

Nursery Tea Sponge Cake

Makes 6 slices

75 g/3 oz/2/3 cup caster (superfine) sugar
3 eggs, at kitchen temperature
75 g/3 oz/¾ cup plain (all-purpose) flour
90 ml/6 tbsp double (heavy) or whipping cream, whipped
45 ml/3 tbsp jam (conserve)
Caster (superfine) sugar, for sprinkling

Line the base and side of a 18 cm/7 in diameter soufflé dish with clingfilm (plastic wrap), allowing it to hang very slightly over the edge. Put the sugar in a bowl and warm, uncovered, on Defrost for 30 seconds. Add the eggs and beat until the mixture froths up and thickens to the consistency of whipped cream. Gently and lightly cut and fold in the flour using a metal spoon. Do not beat or stir. When the ingredients are well combined, transfer to the prepared dish. Cover loosely with kitchen paper and cook on Full for 4 minutes. Allow to stand for 10 minutes, then transfer to a wire rack by holding the clingfilm. When cold, peel away the clingfilm. Split in half and sandwich together with the cream and jam. Sprinkle the top with caster sugar before serving.

Lemon Sponge Cake

Makes 6 slices

Prepare as for Nursery Tea Sponge Cake, but add 10 ml/2 tsp finely grated lemon peel to the warmed egg and sugar mixture immediately before adding the flour. Sandwich together with lemon curd and thick cream.

Orange Sponge Cake

Makes 6 slices

Prepare as for Nursery Tea Sponge Cake, but add 10 ml/2 tsp finely grated orange peel to the warmed egg and sugar mixture immediately before adding the flour. Sandwich together with chocolate spread and thick cream.

Espresso Coffee Cake

Serves 8

250 g/8 oz/2 cups self-raising (self-rising) flour
15 ml/1 tbsp/2 sachets instant espresso coffee powder
125 g/4 oz/½ cup butter or margarine
125 g/4 oz/½ cup dark soft brown sugar
2 eggs, at kitchen temperature
75 ml/5 tbsp cold milk

Line the base and side of an 18 cm/7 in diameter soufflé dish with clingfilm (plastic wrap), allowing it to hang very slightly over the edge. Sift the flour and coffee powder into a bowl and rub in the butter or margarine. Add the sugar. Thoroughly beat together the eggs and milk, then mix evenly into the dry ingredients with a fork. Spoon into the prepared dish and cover loosely with kitchen paper. Cook on Full for 6½–7 minutes until the cake is well risen and just beginning to shrink away from the side of the dish. Allow to stand for 10 minutes. Transfer to a wire rack by holding the clingfilm. When completely cold, peel away the clingfilm and store the cake in an airtight container.

Orange-iced Espresso Coffee Cake

Serves 8

Make the Espresso Coffee Cake. About 2 hours before serving, make up a thick glacé icing (frosting) by mixing 175 g/6 oz/1 cup icing (confectioners') sugar with enough orange juice to form a paste-like icing. Spread over the top of the cake, then decorate with grated chocolate, chopped nuts, hundreds and thousands etc.

Espresso Coffee Cream Torte

Serves 8

Make the Espresso Coffee Cake and cut into two layers. Whip 300 ml/½ pt/1¼ cups double (heavy) cream with 60 ml/4 tbsp cold milk until thick. Sweeten with 45 ml/3 tbsp caster (superfine) sugar and flavour to taste with espresso coffee powder. Use some to sandwich the layers together, then spread the remainder thickly over the top and side of the cake. Stud the top with hazelnuts.

Raisin Cup Cakes

Makes 12

125 g/4 oz/1 cup self-raising (self-rising) flour
50 g/2 oz/¼ cup butter or margarine
50 g/2 oz/¼ cup caster (superfine) sugar
30 ml/2 tbsp raisins
1 egg
30 ml/2 tbsp cold milk
2.5 ml/½ tsp vanilla essence (extract)
Icing (confectioner's) sugar, for dusting

Sift the flour into bowl and rub in the butter or margarine finely. Add the sugar and raisins. Beat the egg with the milk and vanilla essence and stir into the dry ingredients with a fork, mixing to a soft batter without beating. Divide between 12 paper cake cases (cupcake papers) and place six at a time on the microwave turntable. Cover loosely with kitchen paper. Cook on Full for 2 minutes. Transfer to a wire rack to cool. Dust with sifted icing sugar when cold. Store in an airtight container.

Coconut Cup Cakes

Makes 12

Prepare as for Raisin Cup Cakes, but substitute 25 ml/1½ tbsp desiccated (shredded) coconut for the raisins and increase the milk to 25 ml/1½ tbsp.

Chocolate Chip Cakes

Makes 12

Prepare as for Raisin Cup Cakes, but substitute 30 ml/2 tbsp chocolate chips for the raisins.

Banana Spice Cake

Serves 8

3 large ripe bananas
175 g/6 oz/¾ cup mixture of margarine and white cooking fat (shortening), at kitchen temperature
175 g/6 oz/¾ cup dark soft brown sugar
10 ml/2 tsp baking powder
5 ml/1 tsp ground allspice
225 g/8 oz/2 cups malted brown flour, such as granary
1 large egg, beaten
15 ml/1 tbsp chopped pecan nuts
100 g/4 oz/2/3 cup chopped dates

Closely line the base and side of a 20 cm/8 in diameter soufflé dish with clingfilm (plastic wrap), allowing it to hang very slightly over the edge. Peel the bananas and thoroughly mash in a bowl. Beat in both fats. Mix in the sugar. Toss the baking powder and allspice with the flour. Stir into the banana mixture with the egg, nuts and dates using a fork. Spread smoothly into the prepared dish. Cover loosely with kitchen paper and cook on Full for 11 minutes, turning the dish three times. Allow to stand for 10 minutes. Transfer to a wire rack by holding the clingfilm. Cool completely, then peel away the clingfilm and store the cake in an airtight container.

Banana Spice Cake with Pineapple Icing

Serves 8

Make the Banana Spice Cake. About 2 hours before serving, cover the cake with a thick glacé icing (frosting) made by sifting 175 g/6 oz/1 cup icing (confectioners') sugar into a bowl and mixing to a paste-like icing with a few drops of pineapple juice. When set, decorate with dried banana chips.

Butter Cream Icing

Makes 225 g/8 oz/1 cup

75 g/3 oz/1/3 cup butter, at kitchen temperature
175 g/6 oz/1 cup icing (confectioners') sugar, sifted
10 ml/2 tsp cold milk
5 ml/1 tsp vanilla essence (extract)
Icing (confectioners') sugar, for dusting (optional)

Beat the butter until light, then gradually beat in the sugar until light, fluffy and doubled in volume. Mix in the milk and vanilla essence and beat the icing (frosting) until smooth and thick.

Chocolate Fudge Frosting

Makes 350 g/12 oz/1½ cups

An American-style icing (frosting) which is useful for topping any plain cake.

30 ml/2 tbsp butter or margarine
60 ml/4 tbsp milk
30 ml/2 tbsp cocoa (unsweetened chocolate) powder
5 ml/1 tsp vanilla essence (extract)
300 g/10 oz/12/3 cups icing (confectioners') sugar, sifted

Put the butter or margarine, milk, cocoa and vanilla essence in a bowl. Cook, uncovered, on Defrost for 4 minutes until hot and the fat has melted. Beat in the sifted icing sugar until the frosting is smooth and quite thick. Use straight away.

Fruited Health Wedges

Makes 8

100 g/3½ oz dried apple rings
75 g/3 oz/¾ cup self-raising (self-rising) wholemeal flour
75 g/3 oz/¾ cup oatmeal
75 g/3 oz/2/3 cup margarine
75 g/3 oz/2/3 cup dark soft brown sugar
6 California prunes, chopped

Soak the apple rings in water overnight. Closely line the base and side of a shallow 18 cm/7 in diameter dish with clingfilm (plastic wrap), allowing it to hang very slightly over the edge. Put the flour and oatmeal into a bowl, add the margarine and rub in finely with the fingertips. Mix in the sugar to make a crumbly mixture. Spread half over the base of the prepared dish. Drain and chop the apple rings. Gently press with the prunes over the oatmeal mixture. Sprinkle the rest of the oatmeal mixture evenly on top. Cook, uncovered, on Full for 5½–6 minutes. Allow to cool completely in the dish. Lift out by holding the clingfilm, then peel away the clingfilm and cut into wedges. Store in an airtight container.

Fruited Health Wedges with Apricots

Makes 8

Prepare as for Fruited Health Wedges, but

substitute 6 dried apricots, well washed, for the prunes.

Shortbread

Makes 12 wedges

225 g/8 oz/1 cup unsalted (sweet) butter, at kitchen temperature
125 g/4 oz/½ cup caster (superfine) sugar, plus extra for sprinkling
350 g/12 oz/3 cups plain (all-purpose) flour

Grease and base line a 20 cm/8 in diameter deep dish. Cream together the butter and sugar until light and fluffy, then mix in the flour until smooth and evenly combined. Spread smoothly into the prepared dish and prick all over with a fork. Cook, uncovered, on Defrost for 20 minutes. Remove from the microwave and sprinkle with 15 ml/1 tbsp caster sugar. Cut into 12 wedges when still slightly warm. Carefully transfer to a wire rack and allow to cool completely. Store in an airtight container.

Extra Crunchy Shortbread

Makes 12 wedges

Prepare as for Shortbread, but substitute 25 g/1 oz/¼ cup semolina (cream of wheat) for 25 g/1 oz/¼ cup of the flour.

Extra Smooth Shortbread

Makes 12 wedges

Prepare as for Shortbread, but substitute 25 g/1 oz/¼ cup cornflour (cornstarch) for 25 g/1 oz/¼ cup of the flour.

Spicy Shortbread

Makes 12 wedges

Prepare as for Shortbread, but sift in 10 ml/2 tsp mixed (apple-pie) spice with the flour.

Dutch-style Shortbread

Makes 12 wedges

Prepare as for Shortbread, but substitute self-raising (self-rising) flour for the plain flour and sift 10 ml/2 tsp ground cinnamon with the flour. Before cooking, brush the top with 15–30 ml/1–2 tbsp cream, then gently press on lightly toasted flaked (slivered) almonds.

Cinnamon Balls

Makes 20

A Passover Festival speciality, a cross between a biscuit (cookie) and a cake, which seems to behave better in the microwave than it does when baked conventionally.

2 large egg whites
125 g/4 oz/½ cup caster (superfine) sugar
30 ml/2 tbsp ground cinnamon
225 g/8 oz/2 cups ground almonds
Sifted icing (confectioners') sugar

Whip the egg whites until they just begin to foam, then stir in the sugar, cinnamon and almonds. Using damp hands, roll into 20 balls. Arrange in two rings, one just inside the other, round the edge of a large flat plate. Cook, uncovered, on Full for 8 minutes, turning the plate four times. Cool to just warm, then roll in icing sugar until each one is heavily coated. Allow to cool completely and store in an airtight container.

Golden Brandy Snaps

Makes 14

Quite difficult to make conventionally, these work like a dream in the microwave.

50 g/2 oz/¼ cup butter
50 g/2 oz/1/6 cup golden (light corn) syrup
40 g/1½ oz/3 tbsp golden granulated sugar
40 g/1½ oz/1½ tbsp malted brown flour, such as granary
2.5 ml/½ tsp ground ginger
150 ml/¼ pt/2/3 cup double (heavy) or whipping cream, whipped

Put the butter in a dish and melt, uncovered, on Defrost for 2–2½ minutes. Add the syrup and sugar and stir in well. Cook, uncovered, on Full for 1 minute. Stir in the flour and ginger. Place four 5 ml/1 tsp sized spoonfuls of the mixture very well apart directly on to the microwave glass or plastic turntable. Cook on Full for 1½–1¾ minutes until the brandy snaps begin to brown and look lacy on top. Carefully lift the turntable out of the microwave and allow the biscuits (cookies) to stand for 5 minutes. Lift off each one in turn with the help of a palette knife. Roll round the handle of a large wooden spoon. Press the joins together with the fingertips and slide up to the bowl end of the spoon. Repeat with the remaining three biscuits. When they are set, remove from the handle and transfer to a wire cooling rack. Repeat until the remaining mixture is used up. Store in an airtight tin. Before eating, pipe thick cream into both ends of each brandy snap and eat the same day as they soften on standing.

Chocolate Brandy Snaps

Makes 14

Prepare as for Golden Brandy Snaps. Before filling with cream, arrange on a baking sheet and brush the uppermost surface with melted dark or white chocolate. Leave to set, then add the cream.

Bun Scones

Makes about 8

A cross between a bun and a scone, these are exceptionally light and make a delicious treat eaten while still warm, spread with butter and a choice of jam (conserve) or heather honey.

225 g/8 oz/2 cups wholemeal flour
5 ml/1 tsp cream of tartar
5 ml/1 tsp bicarbonate of soda (baking soda)
1.5 ml/¼ tsp salt
20 ml/4 tsp caster (superfine) sugar
25 g/1 oz/2 tbsp butter or margarine
150 ml/¼ pt/2/3 cup buttermilk, or substitute a mixture of half plain yoghurt and half skimmed milk if unavailable
Beaten egg, for brushing
Extra 5 ml/1 tsp sugar mixed with 2.5 ml/½ tsp ground cinnamon, for sprinkling

Sift together the flour, cream of tartar, bicarbonate of soda and salt into a bowl. Toss in the sugar and finely rub in the butter or margarine. Add the buttermilk (or substitute) and mix with a fork to form a fairly soft dough. Turn out on to a floured surface and knead quickly and lightly until smooth. Pat out evenly to 1 cm/½ in thick, then cut into rounds with a 5 cm/2 in biscuit (cookie) cutter. Re-roll the trimmings and continue cutting into rounds. Place round the edge of a buttered 25 cm/10 in flat plate. Brush with egg and sprinkle with the sugar and cinnamon mixture. Cook, uncovered, on Full for 4 minutes, turning the plate four times. Allow to stand for 4 minutes, then transfer to a wire rack. Eat while still warm.

Raisin Bun Scones

Makes about 8

Prepare as for Bun Scones, but add 15 ml/1 tbsp raisins with the sugar.

Breads

Any liquid used in yeasted breads must be lukewarm – not hot or cold. The best way to achieve the correct temperature is to mix half boiling liquid with half cold liquid. If it still feels hot when you dip in the second knuckle of your little finger, cool it down slightly before use. Over-hot liquid is more of a problem than too cold liquid as it can kill off the yeast and stop the bread rising.

Basic White Bread Dough

Makes 1 loaf

A speedy bread dough for those who enjoy baking but are short of time.

450 g/1 lb/4 cups strong plain (bread) flour
5 ml/1 tsp salt
1 sachet easy-blend dried yeast
30 ml/2 tbsp butter, margarine, white cooking fat (shortening) or lard
300 ml/½ pt/1¼ cups lukewarm water

Sift the flour and salt into a bowl. Warm, uncovered, on Defrost for 1 minute. Add the yeast and rub in the fat. Mix to a dough with the water. Knead on a floured surface until smooth, elastic and no longer sticky. Return to the cleaned and dried but now lightly greased bowl. Cover the bowl itself, not the dough, with clingfilm (plastic wrap) and slit it twice to allow steam to escape. Warm on Defrost for 1 minute. Rest in the microwave for 5 minutes. Repeat three or four times until the dough has doubled in size. Quickly re-knead, then use as in conventional recipes or in the microwave recipes below.

Basic Brown Bread Dough

Makes 1 loaf

Follow the recipe for Basic White Bread Dough, but in place of the strong bread (plain) flour use one of the following:
- half white and half wholemeal flour
- all wholemeal flour
- half malted wholemeal and half white flour
-

Basic Milk Bread Dough

Makes 1 loaf

Follow the recipe for Basic White Bread Dough, but in place of the water use one of the following:
- all skimmed milk
- half full-cream milk and half water

Bap Loaf

Makes 1 loaf

A soft crusted and pale loaf, eaten more in the north of Britain than the south.

Make up either the Basic White Bread Dough, Basic Brown Bread Dough or Basic Milk Bread Dough. Knead quickly and lightly after the first rising, then shape into a round about 5 cm/2 in thick. Stand on a greased and floured round flat plate. Cover with kitchen paper and warm on Defrost for 1 minute. Allow to rest for 4 minutes. Repeat three or four times until the dough has doubled in size. Sprinkle with white or brown flour. Cook, uncovered, on Full for 4 minutes. Cool on a wire rack.

Bap Rolls

Makes 16

Make up either the Basic White Bread Dough, Basic Brown Bread Dough or Basic Milk Bread Dough. Knead quickly and lightly after the first rising, then divide equally into 16 pieces. Shape into flattish rounds. Arrange eight baps round the edge of each of two greased and floured plates. Cover with kitchen paper and cook, one plate at a time, on Defrost for 1 minute, then rest for 4 minutes, and repeat three or four times until the rolls have doubled in size. Sprinkle with white or brown flour. Cook, uncovered, on Full for 4 minutes. Cool on a wire rack.

Hamburger Buns

Makes 12

Prepare as for Bap Rolls, but divide the dough into 12 pieces instead of 16. Put six buns round the edge of each of two plates and cook as directed.

Fruited Sweet Bap Rolls

Makes 16

Prepare as for Bap Rolls, but add 60 ml/4 tbsp raisins and 30 ml/2 tbsp caster (superfine) sugar to the dry ingredients before mixing in the liquid.

Cornish Splits

Makes 16

Prepare as for Bap Rolls, but do not sprinkle the tops with flour before cooking. Halve when cold and fill with thick cream or clotted cream and strawberry or raspberry jam (conserve). Dust the tops heavily with sifted icing (confectioners') sugar. Eat the same day.

Fancy Rolls

Makes 16

Make up either the Basic White Bread Dough, Basic Brown Bread Dough or Basic Milk Bread Dough. Knead quickly and lightly after the first rising, then divide equally into 16 pieces. Shape four pieces into round rolls and cut a slit across the top of each. Roll four pieces into ropes, each 20 cm/8 in long, and tie in a knot. Shape four pieces into baby Vienna loaves and make three diagonal slits on top of each. Divide each of the remaining four pieces into three, roll into narrow ropes and plait together. Arrange all the rolls on a greased and floured baking tray and leave in the warm until doubled in size. Brush the tops with egg and bake conventionally at 230°C/450°F/gas mark 8 for 15–20 minutes. Remove from the oven and transfer the rolls to a wire rack. Store in an airtight container when cold.

Rolls with Toppings

Makes 16

Prepare as for Fancy Rolls. After brushing the tops of the rolls with egg, sprinkle with any of the following: poppy seeds, toasted sesame seeds, fennel seeds, porridge oats, cracked wheat, grated hard cheese, coarse sea salt, flavoured seasoning salts.

Caraway Seed Bread

Makes 1 loaf

Make up the Basic Brown Bread Dough, adding 10-15 ml/2–3 tsp caraway seeds to the dry ingredients before mixing in the liquid. Knead lightly after the first rising, then shape into a ball. Put into a 450 ml/¾ pt/2 cup straight-sided greased round dish. Cover with kitchen paper and warm on Defrost for 1 minute. Allow to rest for 4 minutes. Repeat three or four times until the dough has doubled in size. Brush with beaten egg and sprinkle with coarse salt and/or extra caraway seeds. Cover with kitchen paper and cook on Full for 5 minutes, turning the dish once. Cook on Full for a further 2 minutes. Leave for 15 minutes, then carefully turn out on to a wire rack.

Rye Bread

Makes 1 loaf

Make up the Basic Brown Bread Dough, using half wholemeal and half rye flour. Bake as for Bap Loaf.

Oil Bread

Makes 1 loaf

Make up either the Basic White Bread Dough or Basic Brown Bread Dough, but substitute olive, walnut or hazelnut oil for the other fats. If the dough remains on the sticky side, work in a little extra flour. Cook as for Bap Loaf.

Italian Bread

Makes 1 loaf

Make up the Basic White Bread Dough, but substitute olive oil for the other fats and add 15 ml/1 tbsp red pesto and 10 ml/2 tsp sun-dried tomato purée (paste) to the dry ingredients before mixing in the liquid. Cook as for Bap Loaf, allowing an extra 30 seconds.

Spanish Bread

Makes 1 loaf

Make up the Basic White Bread Dough, but substitute olive oil for the other fats and add 30 ml/2 tbsp dried onions (in their dry state) and 12 chopped stuffed olives to the dry ingredients before mixing in the liquid. Cook as for Bap Loaf, allowing an extra 30 seconds.

Tikka Masala Bread

Makes 1 loaf

Make up the Basic White Bread Dough, but substitute melted ghee or corn oil for the other fats and add 15 ml/1 tbsp tikka spice blend and the seeds from 5 green cardamom pods to the dry ingredients before mixing in the liquid. Cook as for Bap Loaf, allowing an extra 30 seconds.

Fruited Malt Bread

Makes 2 loaves

450 g/1 lb/4 cups strong plain (bread) flour
10 ml/2 tsp salt
1 sachet easy-blend dried yeast
60 ml/4 tbsp mixed currants and raisins
60 ml/4 tbsp malt extract
15 ml/1 tbsp black treacle (molasses)
25 g/1 oz/2 tbsp butter or margarine
45 ml/3 tbsp lukewarm skimmed milk
150 ml/¼ pt/2/3 cup lukewarm water
Butter, for spreading

Sift the flour and salt into a bowl. Toss in the yeast and dried fruit. Put the malt extract, treacle and butter or margarine into a small basin. Melt, uncovered, on Defrost for 3 minutes. Add to the flour with the milk and enough water to make a soft but not sticky dough. Knead on a floured surface until smooth, elastic and no longer sticky. Divide into two equal pieces. Shape each to fit a greased 900 ml/1½ pt/3¾ cup round or rectangular dish. Cover the dishes, not the dough, with clingfilm (plastic wrap) and slit it twice to allow steam to escape. Warm together on Defrost for 1 minute. Allow to stand for 5 minutes. Repeat three or four times until the dough has doubled in size. Remove the clingfilm. Place the dishes side by side in the microwave and cook, uncovered, on Full for 2 minutes. Reverse the position of the dishes and cook for a further 2 minutes. Repeat once more. Allow to stand for 10 minutes. Invert on to a wire rack. Store in an airtight container when completely cold. Leave for 1 day before slicing and spreading with butter.

Irish Soda Bread

Makes 4 small loaves

200 ml/7 fl oz/scant 1 cup buttermilk or 60 ml/4 tbsp each skimmed milk and plain yoghurt
75 ml/5 tbsp full-cream milk
350 g/12 oz/3 cups wholemeal flour
125 g/4 oz/1 cup plain (all-purpose) flour
10 ml/2 tsp bicarbonate of soda (baking soda)
5 ml/1 tsp cream of tartar
5 ml/1 tsp salt
50 g/2 oz/¼ cup butter, margarine or white cooking fat (shortening)

Thoroughly grease a 25 cm/10 in dinner plate. Mix together the buttermilk or substitute and milk. Tip the wholemeal flour into a bowl and sift in the plain flour, bicarbonate of soda, cream of tartar and salt. Rub the fat in finely. Add the liquid in one go and stir to a soft dough with a fork. Knead quickly with floured hands until smooth. Shape into an 18 cm/7 in round. Transfer to the centre of the plate. Cut a deepish cross on the top with the back of a knife, then dust lightly with flour. Cover loosely with kitchen paper and cook on Full for 7 minutes. The bread will rise and spread. Allow to stand for 10 minutes. Lift off the plate with the help of a fish slice and place on a wire rack. Divide into four portions when cold. Store in an airtight container for up to only 2 days as this type of bread is best eaten fresh.

Soda Bread with Bran

Makes 4 small loaves

Prepare as for Irish Soda Bread, but add 60 ml/4 tbsp coarse bran before mixing in the liquid.

To Freshen Stale Bread

Put the bread or rolls in a brown paper bag or place between the folds of a clean tea towel (dish cloth) or table napkin. Heat on Defrost until the bread feels slightly warm on the surface. Eat straight away and don't repeat with leftovers of the same bread.

Greek Pittas

Makes 4 loaves

Make up the Basic White Bread Dough. Divide into four equal pieces and knead each lightly into a ball. Roll into ovals, each 30 cm/12 in long down the centre. Dust lightly with flour. Dampen the edges with water. Fold each in half by bringing the top edge over the bottom. Press the edges well together to seal. Place on a greased and floured baking sheet. Bake straight away in a conventional oven at 230°C/450°F/gas mark 8 for 20–25 minutes until the loaves are well risen and a deep golden brown. Cool on a wire rack. Leave until just cold, then split open and eat with Greek-style dips and other foods.

Jellied Cherries in Port

Serves 6

750 g/1½ lb canned stoned (pitted) morello cherries in light syrup, drained and syrup reserved
15 ml/1 tbsp powdered gelatine
45 ml/3 tbsp caster (superfine) sugar
2.5 ml/½ tsp ground cinnamon
Tawny port
Double (heavy) cream, whipped, and mixed (apple-pie) spice, to decorate

Pour 30 ml/2 tbsp of the syrup into a large measuring jug. Stir in the gelatine and leave for 2 minutes to soften. Cover with a saucer and melt on Defrost for 2 minutes. Stir to ensure the gelatine has melted. Mix in the remaining cherry syrup, the sugar and cinnamon. Make up to 450 ml/¾ pt/2 cups with port. Cover as before and heat on Full for 2 minutes, stirring three times, until the liquid is warm and the sugar has dissolved. Transfer to a 1.25 litre/2¼ pt/5½ cup basin and allow to cool. Cover and chill until the jelly mixture is beginning to thicken and set slightly round the side of the basin. Fold in the cherries and divide between six dessert dishes. Chill until completely set. Decorate with thick cream and a dusting of mixed spice before serving.

Jellied Cherries in Cider

Serves 6

Prepare as for Jellied Cherries in Port, but substitute strong dry cider for the port and 5 ml/1 tsp grated orange peel for the cinnamon.

Mulled Pineapple

Serves 8

225 g/8 oz/1 cup caster (superfine) sugar
150 ml/¼ pt/2/3 cup cold water
1 large fresh pineapple
6 whole cloves
5 cm/2 in piece cinnamon stick
1.5 ml/¼ tsp grated nutmeg
60 ml/4 tbsp medium-dry sherry
15 ml/1 tbsp dark rum
Biscuits (cookies), to serve

Put the sugar and water in a 2.5 litre/4½ pt/11 cup dish and stir well. Cover with a large inverted plate and cook on Full for 8 minutes to make a syrup. Meanwhile, peel and core the pineapple and remove the 'eyes' with the tip of a potato peeler. Cut into slices, then cut the slices into chunks. Add to the syrup with the remaining ingredients. Cover with clingfilm (plastic wrap) and slit it twice to allow steam to escape. Cook on Full for 10 minutes, turning the dish three times. Allow to stand for 8 minutes before spooning into dishes and eating with crisp, buttery biscuits.

Mulled Sharon Fruit

Serves 8

Prepare as for Mulled Pineapple, but substitute 8 quartered sharon fruit for the pineapple. After adding to the syrup with the other ingredients, cook on Full for only 5 minutes. Flavour with brandy instead of rum.

Mulled Peaches

Serves 8

Prepare as for Mulled Pineapple, but substitute 8 large halved and stoned (pitted) peaches for the pineapple. After adding to the syrup with the other ingredients, cook on Full for only 5 minutes. Flavour with an orange liqueur instead of rum.

Pink Pears

Serves 6

450 ml/¾ pt/2 cups rosé wine
75 g/3 oz/1/3 cup caster (superfine) sugar
6 dessert pears, stalks left on
30 ml/2 tbsp cornflour (cornstarch)
45 ml/3 tbsp cold water
45 ml/3 tbsp tawny port

Pour the wine into a deep dish large enough to hold all the pears on their sides in a single layer. Add the sugar and stir in well. Cook, uncovered, on Full for 3 minutes. Meanwhile, peel the pears, taking care not to lose the stalks. Arrange on their sides in the wine and sugar mixture. Cover with clingfilm (plastic wrap) and slit it twice to allow steam to escape. Cook on Full for 4 minutes. Turn the pears over with two spoons. Cover as before and cook on Full for a further 4 minutes. Allow to stand for 5 minutes. Rearrange upright in the serving dish. To thicken the sauce, mix the cornflour smoothly with the water and stir in the port. Blend into the wine mixture. Cook, uncovered, on Full for 5 minutes, stirring briskly every minute until lightly thickened and clear. Pour over the pears and serve warm or chilled.

Christmas Pudding

Makes 2 puddings, each serving 6–8

65 g/2½ oz plain (all-purpose) flour
15 ml/1 tbsp cocoa (unsweetened chocolate) powder
10 ml/2 tsp mixed (apple-pie) spice or ground allspice
5 ml/1 tsp grated orange or tangerine peel
75 g/3 oz/1½ cups fresh brown breadcrumbs
125 g/4 oz/½ cup dark soft brown sugar
450 g/1 lb/4 cups mixed dried fruit (fruit cake mix) with peel
125 g/4 oz/1 cup shredded suet (vegetarian if preferred)
2 large eggs, at kitchen temperature
15 ml/1 tbsp black treacle (molasses)
60 ml/4 tbsp Guinness
15 ml/1 tbsp milk

Thoroughly grease two 900 ml/1½ pt/3¾ cup pudding basins. Sift the flour, cocoa and spice into a large bowl. Toss in the peel, breadcrumbs, sugar, fruit and suet. In a separate bowl, beat together the eggs, treacle, Guinness and milk. Stir into the dry ingredients with a fork to make a softish mixture. Divide equally between the prepared basins. Cover each loosely with kitchen paper. Cook, one at a time, on Full for 4 minutes. Allow to stand for 3 minutes inside the microwave. Cook each pudding on Full for a further 2 minutes. Turn out of the basins when cool. When cold, wrap with a double thickness of greaseproof (waxed) paper and freeze until needed. To serve, defrost completely, cut into portions and reheat individually on plates for 50–60 seconds.

Butter Plum Pudding

Makes 2 puddings, each serving 6–8

Prepare as for Christmas Pudding, but substitute 125 g/4 oz/½ cup melted butter for the suet.

Plum Pudding with Oil

Makes 2 puddings, each serving 6–8

Prepare as for Christmas Pudding, but substitute 75 ml/5 tbsp sunflower or corn oil for the suet. Add an extra 15 ml/1 tbsp milk.

Fruit Soufflé in Glasses

Serves 6

400 g/14 oz/1 large can any fruit filling

3 eggs, separated

90 ml/6 tbsp unbeaten whipping cream

Spoon the fruit filling into a bowl and stir in the egg yolks. Beat the whites to stiff peaks and fold lightly into the fruit mixture until thoroughly combined. Spoon the mixture equally into six stemmed wine glasses (not crystal) until half-filled. Cook in pairs on Defrost for 3 minutes. The mixture should rise to the top of each glass, but will drop slightly when removed from the oven. Make a slit in top of each with a knife. Spoon 15 ml/1 tbsp of the cream on to each. It will flow down the sides of the glasses to the bases. Serve straight away.

Almost Instant Christmas Pudding

Makes 2 puddings, each serving 8

Absolutely superb, amazingly rich-tasting, deep-toned, fruity and quick to mature so they don't have to be made weeks ahead. Canned fruit filling is the prime mover here and accounts for the unfailing success of the puddings.

225 g/8 oz/4 cups fresh white breadcrumbs
125 g/4 oz/1 cup plain (all-purpose) flour
12.5 ml/2½ tsp ground allspice
175 g/6 oz/¾ cup dark soft brown sugar
275 g/10 oz/2¼ cups finely shredded suet (vegetarian if preferred)
675 g/1½ lb/4 cups mixed dried fruit (fruit cake mix)
3 eggs, thoroughly beaten
400 g/14 oz/1 large can cherry fruit filling
30 ml/2 tbsp black treacle (molasses)
Dutch Butter Blender Cream or whipped cream, to serve.

Thoroughly grease two 900 ml/1½ pt/3¾ cup pudding basins. Place the breadcrumbs into a bowl and sift in the flour and allspice. Add the sugar, suet and dried fruit. Mix to a fairly soft mixture with the eggs, fruit filling and treacle. Divide between the prepared basins and cover each loosely with kitchen paper. Cook, one at a time, on Full for 6 minutes. Allow to stand for 5 minutes inside the microwave. Cook each pudding on Full for a further 3 minutes, turning the basin twice. Turn out of the basins when cool. When cold, wrap in greaseproof (waxed) paper and refrigerate until needed. Cut into portions and reheat as directed in the Convenience Foods table. Serve with the blender cream or whipped cream.

Ultra-fruity Christmas Pudding

Serves 8–10

An oldie from Billington's Sugar, with butter or margarine replacing sugar.

75 g/3 oz/¾ cup plain (all-purpose) flour
7.5 ml/1½ tsp ground allspice
40 g/1½ oz/¾ cup wholemeal breadcrumbs
75 g/3 oz/1/3 cup demerara sugar
75 g/3 oz/1/3 molasses sugar
125 g/4 oz/2/3 cup currants
125 g/4 oz/2/3 cup sultanas (golden raisins)
125 g/4 oz/2/3 cup dried apricots, snipped into small pieces
45 ml/3 tbsp chopped roasted hazelnuts
1 small eating (dessert) apple, peeled and grated
Finely grated peel and juice of 1 small orange
50 ml/2 fl oz/3½ tbsp cold milk
75 g/3 oz/1/3 cup butter or margarine
50 g/2 oz plain (semi-sweet) chocolate, broken into pieces
1 large egg, beaten
Brandy Sauce

Thoroughly butter a 900 ml/1½ pt/3¾ cup pudding basin. Sift the flour and spice into a large bowl. Add the breadcrumbs and sugars and toss to ensure any lumps are broken down. Mix in the dried currants, sultanas, apricots, nuts, apple and orange peel. Pour the orange juice into a jug. Add the milk, butter or margarine and the chocolate. Heat on Defrost for 2½–3 minutes until the butter and chocolate have melted. Fork into the dry ingredients with the beaten egg. Spoon into the prepared basin. Cover loosely with a round of parchment or greaseproof (waxed) paper. Cook on Full for 5 minutes, turning the basin twice. Allow to stand for 5 minutes. Cook on Full for a further 5 minutes, turning the basin twice. Allow to stand for 5 minutes before inverting on to a plate and serving with Brandy Sauce.

Plum Crumble

Serves 4

450 g/1 lb stoned (pitted) plums
125 g/4 oz/½ cup soft brown sugar
175 g/6 oz/1½ cups plain (all-purpose) wholemeal flour
125 g/4 oz/½ cup butter or margarine
75 g/3 oz/1/3 cup demerara sugar
2.5 ml/½ tsp ground allspice (optional)

Place the plums in a buttered 1 litre/1¾ pt/4¼ cup pie dish. Mix in the sugar. Tip the flour into bowl and rub in the butter or margarine finely. Add the sugar and spice and toss together. Sprinkle the mixture thickly over the fruit. Cook, uncovered, on Full for 10 minutes, turning the dish twice. Allow to stand for 5 minutes. Eat hot or warm.

Plum and Apple Crumble

Serves 4

Prepare as for Plum Crumble, but substitute 225 g/8 oz peeled and sliced apples for half the plums. Add 5 ml/1 tsp grated lemon peel to the fruit with the sugar.

Apricot Crumble

Serves 4

Prepare as for Plum Crumble, but substitute stoned (pitted) fresh apricots for the plums.

Berry Fruit Crumble with Almonds

Serves 4

Prepare as for Plum Crumble, but substitute prepared mixed berry fruits for the plums. Add 30 ml/2 tbsp toasted flaked (slivered) almonds to the crumble mixture.

Pear and Rhubarb Crumble

Serves 4

Prepare as for Plum Crumble, but substitute a mixture of peeled and chopped pears and chopped rhubarb for the plums.

Nectarine and Blueberry Crumble

Serves 4

Prepare as for Plum Crumble, but substitute a mixture of stoned (pitted) and sliced nectarines and blueberries for the plums.

Apple Betty

Serves 4–6

50 g/2 oz/¼ cup butter or margarine
125 g/4 oz/2 cups crisp breadcrumbs, bought or made from toast
175 g/6 oz/¾ cup light soft brown sugar
750 g/1½ lb cooking (tart) apples, peeled, cored and thinly sliced
30 ml/2 tbsp lemon juice
Grated zest of 1 small lemon
2.5 ml/½ tsp ground cinnamon
75 ml/5 tbsp cold water
Double (heavy) cream, whipped, or ice cream, to serve

Butter a 600 ml/1 pt/2½ cup pie dish. Melt the butter or margarine on Full for 45 seconds. Stir in the breadcrumbs and two-thirds of the sugar. Combine the apple slices, lemon juice, lemon zest, cinnamon, water and remaining sugar. Fill the prepared pie dish with alternate layers of the breadcrumb and apple mixtures, beginning and ending with breadcrumbs. Cook, uncovered, on Full for 7 minutes, turning the dish twice. Allow to stand for 5 minutes before eating with thick cream or ice cream.

Nectarine or Peach Betty

Serves 4–6

Prepare as for Apple Betty, but substitute sliced stoned (pitted) nectarines or peaches for the apples.

Middle Eastern Shred Pudding with Nuts

Serves 6

This is a fine pudding from what was once known as Arabia. The orange flower water is available from some supermarkets and pharmacies.

6 large Shredded Wheats
100 g/3½ oz/1 cup toasted pine nuts
125 g/4 oz/½ cup caster (superfine) sugar
150 ml/¼ pt/2/3 cup full-cream milk
50 g/2 oz/¼ cup butter (not margarine)
45 ml/3 tbsp orange flower water

Butter a deep 20 cm/8 in diameter dish and crumble 3 of the Shredded Wheats across the base. Combine the nuts and sugar and sprinkle evenly on top. Crush over the remaining Shredded Wheats. Heat the milk and butter in a jug, uncovered, on Full for 1½ minutes. Mix in the orange flower water. Spoon gently over the ingredients in the dish. Cook, uncovered, on Full for 6 minutes. Allow to stand for 2 minutes before serving.

Cocktail of Summer Fruits

Serves 8

225 g/8 oz/2 cups gooseberries, topped and tailed
225 g/8 oz rhubarb, chopped
30 ml/2 tbsp cold water
250 g/8 oz/1 cup caster (superfine) sugar
450 g/1 lb strawberries, sliced
125 g/4 oz raspberries
125 g/4 oz redcurrants, stalks removed
30 ml/2 tbsp Cassis or orange liqueur (optional)

Put the gooseberries and rhubarb into a deep dish with the water. Cover with clingfilm (plastic wrap) and slit it twice to allow steam to escape. Cook on Full for 6 minutes, turning the dish once. Uncover. Add the sugar and stir until dissolved. Mix in the remaining fruit. Cover when cold and chill thoroughly. Add the Cassis or liqueur, if using, just before serving.

Middle Eastern Date and Banana Compôte

Serves 6

Fresh dates, usually from Israel, are readily available in the winter.

> 450 g/1 lb fresh dates
> 450 g/1 lb bananas
> Juice of ½ lemon
> Juice of ½ orange
> 45 ml/3 tbsp orange or apricot brandy
> 15 ml/1 tbsp rose water
> 30 ml/2 tbsp demerara sugar
> Sponge cake, to serve

Skin the dates and slit in half to remove the stones (pits). Place in a 1.75 litre/3 pt/7½ cup serving bowl. Peel the bananas and slice directly on to the top. Add all the remaining ingredients and toss gently to mix. Cover with clingfilm (plastic wrap) and slit it twice to allow steam to escape. Cook on Full for 6 minutes, turning the dish twice. Eat warm with sponge cake.

Mixed Dried Fruit Salad

Serves 4

225 g/8 oz mixed dried fruits such as apple rings, apricots, peaches, pears, prunes
300 ml/½ pt/1¼ cups boiling water
50 g/2 oz/¼ cup granulated sugar
10 ml/2 tsp finely grated lemon peel
Thick plain yoghurt, to serve

Wash the fruit thoroughly and place in a 1.25 litre/2¼ pt/5½ cup bowl. Stir in the water and sugar. Cover with a plate and leave to soak for 4 hours. Transfer to the microwave and cook on Full for about 20 minutes until the fruit is tender. Stir in the lemon peel and serve warm with thick yoghurt.

Stodgy Apple and Blackberry Pudding

Serves 6

A little melted butter
275 g/10 oz/2¼ cups self-raising (self-rising) flour
150 g/5 oz/2/3 cup butter or margarine, at kitchen temperature
125 g/4 oz/½ cup soft brown sugar
2 eggs, beaten
400 g/14 oz/1 large can apple and blackberry fruit filling
45 ml/3 tbsp cold milk
Cream or custard, to serve

Brush a 1.25 litre/2¼ pt/5½ cup round soufflé dish with the melted butter. Sift the flour into a bowl and rub in the butter or margarine finely. Add the sugar and mix to a soft consistency with the eggs, fruit filling and milk, stirring briskly without beating. Spread evenly into the prepared dish. Cook, uncovered, on Full for 9 minutes, turning the dish three times. Allow to stand for 5 minutes. Turn out into a warmed shallow dish. Spoon on to plates to serve with cream or custard.

Lemony Bramble Pudding

Serves 4

A little melted butter
225g/8 oz/2 cups blackberries, crushed
Finely grated peel and juice of 1 lemon
225 g/8 oz/2 cups self-raising (self-rising) flour
125 g/4 oz/½ cup butter or margarine
100 g/3½ oz/scant ½ cup dark soft brown sugar
2 eggs, beaten
60 ml/4 tbsp cold milk
Cream, ice cream or lemon sorbet, to serve

Brush a deep 18 cm/7 in diameter dish with melted butter. Combine the blackberries with the lemon peel and juice and set aside. Sift the flour into a bowl. Rub in the butter and sugar. Mix to a softish consistency with the crushed fruit, eggs and milk. Spread smoothly into the prepared dish. Cook, uncovered, on Full for 7–8 minutes until the pudding has risen to the top of the dish and the top has no shiny patches. Allow to stand for 5 minutes during which time the pudding will drop slightly. Loosen edges with a knife and turn out on to a warmed plate. Eat warm with cream, ice cream or lemon sorbet.

Lemony Raspberry Pudding

Serves 4

Prepare as for Lemony Bramble Pudding, but substitute raspberries for the blackberries.

Apricot and Walnut Upside-down Pudding

Serves 8

For the pudding:
50 g/2 oz/¼ cup butter or margarine
50 g/2 oz/¼ cup light soft brown sugar
400 g/14 oz canned apricot halves in syrup, drained and syrup reserved
50 g/2 oz/½ cup walnut halves

For the topping:
225 g/8 oz/2 cups self-raising (self-rising) flour
125 g/4 oz/½ cup butter or margarine
125 g/4 oz/½ cup caster (superfine) sugar
Finely grated peel of 1 orange
2 eggs
75 ml/5 tbsp cold milk
2.5–5 ml/½–1 tsp almond essence (extract)
Coffee ice cream, to serve

To make the pudding, butter the base and sides of a deep 25 cm/10 in diameter dish. Add the butter or margarine. Melt, uncovered, on Defrost for 2 minutes. Sprinkle the brown sugar over the butter so that it almost covers the base of the dish. Arrange the apricot halves attractively on top of the sugar, cut sides facing, and intersperse them with the walnut halves.

To make the topping, sift the flour into a bowl. Finely rub in the butter or margarine. Add the sugar and orange peel and toss to combine. Thoroughly beat together the remaining ingredients, then fork into the dry ingredients until evenly mixed. Spread smoothly over the fruit and nuts. Cook, uncovered, on Full for 10 minutes. Allow to stand for 5 minutes, then turn out carefully into a shallow dish. Heat the reserved syrup on Full for 25 seconds. Serve the pudding with coffee ice cream and the warm syrup.

Bananas Foster

Serves 4

From New Orleans and named after Dick Foster, who was in charge of cleaning up the city's morals in the 1950s. Or so the story goes.

25 g/1 oz/2 tbsp butter or sunflower margarine
4 bananas
45 ml/3 tbsp dark soft brown sugar
1.5 ml/¼ tsp ground cinnamon
5 ml/1 tsp finely grated orange peel
60 ml/4 tbsp dark rum
Vanilla ice cream, to serve

Place the butter in a deep 23 cm/9 in diameter dish. Melt on Defrost for 1½ minutes. Peel the bananas, halve lengthways, then cut each half into two pieces. Arrange in the dish and sprinkle with the sugar, cinnamon and orange peel. Cover with clingfilm (plastic wrap) and slit it twice to allow steam to escape. Cook on Full for 3 minutes. Allow to stand for 1 minute. Heat the rum on Defrost until just warm. Ignite the rum with a match and pour over the uncovered bananas. Serve with rich vanilla ice cream.

Mississippi Spice Pie

Serves 8

For the flan case (pie shell):
225 g/8 oz ready-prepared shortcrust pastry (basic pie crust)
1 egg yolk

For the filling:
450 g/1 lb yellow-fleshed pink-skinned sweet potatoes, peeled and cubed
60 ml/4 tbsp boiling water
75 g/3 oz/1/3 cup caster (superfine) sugar
10 ml/2 tsp ground allspice
3 large eggs
150 ml/¼ pt/2/3 cup cold milk
30 ml/2 tbsp melted butter
Whipped cream or vanilla ice cream, to serve

To make the flan case, roll out the pastry thinly and use to line a lightly buttered 23 cm/9 in diameter fluted flan dish. Prick well all over with a fork, especially where the side joins the base. Cook, uncovered, on Full for 6 minutes, turning the dish three times. If bulges appear, gently press down with fingers protected by oven gloves. Brush all over with the egg yolk to seal holes. Cook, uncovered, on Full for a further 1 minute. Set aside.

To make the filling, put the potatoes in a 1 litre/1¾ pt/4¼ cup dish. Add the boiling water. Cover with clingfilm (plastic wrap) and slit it twice to allow steam to escape. Cook on Full for 10 minutes, turning the dish twice. Allow to stand for 5 minutes. Drain. Put into a food processor or blender and add the remaining ingredients. Work to a smooth purée. Spread evenly in the baked pastry case. Cook, uncovered, on Defrost for 20–25 minutes until the filling has set, turning the dish four times. Cool to lukewarm. Cut into portions and serve with softly whipped cream or vanilla ice cream.

Jamaica Pudding

Serves 4–5

225 g/8 oz/2 cups self-raising (self-rising) flour
125 g/4 oz/½ cup mixture white cooking fat (shortening) and margarine
125 g/4 oz/½ cup caster (superfine) sugar
2 large eggs, beaten
50 g/2 oz/¼ cup canned crushed pineapple with syrup
15 ml/1 tbsp coffee and chicory essence (extract) or coffee liqueur
Clotted cream, to serve

Butter a 1.75 litre/3 pt/7½ cup soufflé dish. Sift the flour into a bowl and rub in the fats finely. Mix in the sugar. Mix with a fork to a soft consistency with the eggs, pineapple with syrup and coffee essence or liqueur. Spread smoothly into the dish. Cook, uncovered, on Full for 6 minutes, turning the dish once. Invert on to a serving plate and leave to stand for 5 minutes. Return to the microwave. Cook on Full for a further 1–1½ minutes. Serve with clotted cream.

Pumpkin Pie

Serves 8

Eaten in North America on the last Thursday of every November to celebrate Thanksgiving.

For the flan case (pie shell):
225 g/8 oz ready-prepared shortcrust pastry (basic pie crust)
1 egg yolk

For the filling:
½ small pumpkin or a 1.75 kg/4 lb portion, seeded
30 ml/2 tbsp black treacle (molasses)
175 g/6 oz/¾ cup light soft brown sugar
15 ml/1 tbsp cornflour (cornstarch)
10 ml/2 tsp ground allspice
150 ml/¼ pt/2/3 cup double (heavy) cream
3 eggs, beaten
Whipped cream, to serve

To make the flan case, roll out the pastry thinly and use to line a lightly buttered 23 cm/9 in diameter fluted flan dish. Prick well all over with a fork, especially where the side joins the base. Cook, uncovered, on Full for 6 minutes, turning the dish three times. If bulges appear, gently press down with fingers protected by oven gloves. Brush all over with the egg yolk to seal holes. Cook, uncovered, on Full for a further 1 minute. Set aside.

To make the filling, put the pumpkin on a plate. Cook, uncovered, on Full for 15–18 minutes until the flesh is very soft. Spoon away from the skin and leave to cool to lukewarm. Blend until smooth with the remaining ingredients. Spoon into the pastry case still in its dish. Cook, uncovered, on Full for 20–30 minutes until the filling is set, turning the dish four times. Serve warm with whipped cream. If preferred, use 425 g/15 oz/2 cups canned pumpkin instead of fresh.

Oaten Syrup Tart

Serves 6–8

An up-to-date version of treacle tart.

For the flan case (pie shell):
225 g/8 oz ready-prepared shortcrust pastry (basic pie crust)
1 egg yolk

For the filling:
125 g/4 oz/2 cups toasted muesli with fruit and nuts
75 ml/5 tbsp golden (light corn) syrup
15 ml/1 tbsp black treacle (molasses)
Whipped cream, to serve

To make the flan case, roll out the pastry thinly and use to line a lightly buttered 23 cm/9 in diameter fluted flan dish. Prick well all over with a fork, especially where the side joins the base. Cook, uncovered, on Full for 6 minutes, turning the dish three times. If bulges appear, gently press down with fingers protected by oven gloves. Brush all over with the egg yolk to seal holes. Cook, uncovered, on Full for a further 1 minute. Set aside.

To make the filling, mix together the muesli, syrup and treacle and spoon into the baked flan case. Cook, uncovered, on Full for 3 minutes. Allow to stand for 2 minutes. Cook, uncovered, on Full for a further 1 minute. Serve with cream.

Coconut Sponge Flan

Serves 8–10

For the flan case (pie shell):
225 g/8 oz ready-prepared shortcrust pastry (basic pie crust)
1 egg yolk

For the filling:
175 g/6 oz/1½ cups self-raising (self-rising) flour
75 g/3 oz/1/3 cup butter or margarine
75 g/3 oz/1/3 cup caster (superfine) sugar
75 ml/5 tbsp desiccated (shredded) coconut
2 eggs
5 ml/1 tsp vanilla essence (extract)
60 ml/4 tbsp cold milk
30 ml/2 tbsp strawberry or blackcurrant jam (conserve)

For the icing (frosting):
225 g/8 oz/1 1/3 cups icing (confectioners') sugar, sifted
Orange flower water

To make the flan case, roll out the pastry thinly and use to line a lightly buttered 23 cm/9 in diameter fluted flan dish. Prick well all over with a fork, especially where the side joins the base. Cook, uncovered, on Full for 6 minutes, turning the dish three times. If bulges appear, gently press down with fingers protected by oven gloves. Brush all over with the egg yolk to seal holes. Cook, uncovered, on Full for a further 1 minute. Set aside.

To make the coconut filling, sift the flour into a mixing bowl. Rub in the butter or margarine. Toss in the sugar and coconut, then mix to a soft batter with the eggs, vanilla and milk. Spread the jam over the pastry case still in its dish. Spread evenly with the coconut mixture. Cook, uncovered, on Full for 6 minutes, turning the dish four times. The flan is ready when the top looks dry and no sticky patches remain. Allow to cool completely.

To make the icing, mix the icing sugar with enough orange flower water to make thickish icing; a few teaspoonfuls should be ample. Spread over the top of the flan. Leave until set before cutting.

Easy Bakewell Tart

Serves 8–10

Prepare as for Coconut Sponge Flan, but use raspberry jam (conserve) and substitute ground almonds for the coconut.

Crumbly Mincemeat Pie

Serves 8–10

For the flan case (pie shell):
225 g/8 oz ready-prepared shortcrust pastry (basic pie crust)
1 egg yolk

For the filling:
350 g/12 oz/1 cup mincemeat

For the nut crumble:
50 g/2 oz/¼ cup butter
125 g/4 oz/1 cup self-raising (self-rising) flour, sifted
50 g/2 oz/¼ cup demerara sugar
5 ml/1 tsp ground cinnamon
60 ml/4 tbsp finely chopped walnuts

To serve:
Whipped cream, custard or ice cream

To make the flan case, roll out the pastry thinly and use to line a lightly buttered 23 cm/9 in diameter fluted flan dish. Prick well all over with a fork, especially where the side joins the base. Cook, uncovered, on Full for 6 minutes, turning the dish three times. If bulges appear, gently press down with fingers protected by oven gloves. Brush all over with the egg yolk to seal holes. Cook, uncovered, on Full for a further 1 minute. Set aside.

To make the filling, spoon the mincemeat evenly into the baked flan case.

To make the nut crumble, rub the butter into the flour, then stir in the sugar, cinnamon and walnuts. Press over the mincemeat in an even layer. Leave uncovered and cook on Full for 4 minutes, turning the pie twice. Leave to stand for 5 minutes. Cut into wedges and serve hot with whipped cream, custard or ice cream.

Bread and Butter Pudding

Serves 4

Britain's favourite pudding.

4 large slices white bread
50 g/2 oz/¼ cup butter at kitchen temperature or soft butter spread
50 g/2 oz/1/3 cup currants
50 g/2 oz/¼ cup caster (superfine) sugar
600 ml/1 pt/2½ cups cold milk
3 eggs
30 ml/2 tbsp demerara sugar
Grated nutmeg

Leave the crusts on the bread. Spread each slice with the butter, then cut into four squares. Thoroughly butter a deep 1.75 litre/3 pt/7½ cup square or oval dish. Arrange half the bread squares over the base, buttered sides up. Sprinkle with the currants and caster sugar. Cover with the remaining bread, again buttered sides up. Pour the milk into a jug or bowl. Warm, uncovered, on Full for 3 minutes. Thoroughly beat in the eggs. Slowly and gently pour over the bread. Sprinkle with the demerara sugar and nutmeg. Allow to stand for 30 minutes, loosely covered with a piece of greaseproof (waxed) paper. Cook, uncovered, on Defrost for 30 minutes. Crisp the top under a hot grill (broiler) before serving.

Lemon Curd Bread and Butter Pudding

Serves 4

Prepare as for Bread and Butter Pudding, but spread the bread with Lemon Curd instead of butter.

Baked Egg Custard

Serves 4

Superb eaten on its own, with any kind of fruit salad combination or Cocktail of Summer Fruits.

300 ml/½ pt/1¼ cups single (light) cream or full-cream milk

3 eggs

1 egg yolk

100 g/3½ oz/scant ½ cup caster (superfine) sugar

5 ml/1 tsp vanilla essence (extract)

2.5 ml/½ tsp grated nutmeg

Thoroughly butter a 1 litre/1¾ pt/4¼ cup dish. Pour the cream or milk into a jug. Heat, uncovered, on Full for 1½ minutes. Whisk in all the remaining ingredients except the nutmeg. Strain into a dish. Stand in a second 2 litre/3½ pt/8½ cup dish. Pour boiling water into the larger dish until it reaches the level of the custard in the smaller dish. Sprinkle the top of the custard with the nutmeg. Cook, uncovered, on Full for 6–8 minutes until the custard is only just set. Remove from the microwave and allow to stand for 7 minutes. Lift the dish of custard out of the larger dish and continue to stand until the centre firms up. Serve warm or cold.

Semolina Pudding

Serves 4

Nursery food but still popular with everyone.

50 g/2 oz/1/3 cup semolina (cream of wheat)
50 g/2 oz/¼ cup caster (superfine) sugar
600 ml/1 pt/2½ cups milk
10 ml/2 tsp butter or margarine

Put the semolina in a mixing bowl. Blend in the sugar and milk. Cook, uncovered, on Full for 7–8 minutes, whisking thoroughly every minute, until boiling and thickened. Stir in the butter or margarine. Transfer to serving dishes to eat.

Ground Rice Pudding

Serves 4

Prepare as for Semolina Pudding, but substitute ground rice for the semolina (cream of wheat).

Steamed Suet Treacle Pudding

Serves 4

45 ml/3 tbsp golden (light corn) syrup
125 g/4 oz/1 cup self-raising (self-rising) flour
50 g/2 oz/½ cup shredded suet (vegetarian if preferred)
50 g/2 oz/¼ cup caster (superfine) sugar
1 egg
5 ml/1 tsp vanilla essence (extract)
90 ml/6 tbsp cold milk

Thoroughly grease a 1.25 litre/2¼ pt/5½ cup pudding basin. Pour in the syrup until it covers the base. Sift the flour into a bowl and toss in the suet and sugar. Thoroughly beat together the egg, vanilla essence and milk, then fork into the dry ingredients. Spoon into the basin. Cook, uncovered, on Full for 4–4½ minutes until the pudding has risen to reach the top of the basin. Allow to stand for 2 minutes. Turn out and spoon on to four plates. Serve with any sweet dessert sauce.

Marmalade or Honey Pudding

Serves 4

Prepare as for Steamed Suet Treacle Pudding, but substitute marmalade or honey for the syrup.

Ginger Pudding

Serves 4

Prepare as for Steamed Suet Treacle Pudding, but sift 10 ml/2 tsp ground ginger in with the flour.

Jam Sponge Pudding

Serves 4

45 ml/3 tbsp raspberry jam (conserve)
175 g/6 oz/1½ cups self-raising (self-rising) flour
75 g/3 oz/1/3 cup butter or margarine
75 g/3 oz/1/3 cup caster (superfine) sugar
2 eggs
45 ml/3 tbsp cold milk
5 ml/1 tsp vanilla essence (extract)
Whipped cream or custard, to serve

Spoon the jam into a thoroughly greased 1.5 litre/2½ pt/6 cup pudding basin. Sift the flour into a bowl. Rub in the butter or margarine finely, then toss in the sugar. Thoroughly beat together the eggs, milk and vanilla essence, then fork into the dry ingredients. Spoon into the basin. Cook on Full for 7–8 minutes until the pudding has risen to the top of the basin. Allow to stand for 3 minutes. Turn out and spoon portions on to four plates. Serve with cream or custard.

Lemon Sponge Pudding

Serves 4

Prepare as for Jam Sponge Pudding, but substitute lemon curd for the jam (conserve) and add the finely grated peel of 1 small lemon to the dry ingredients.

Crêpes Suzette

Serves 4

Back in fashion after a long spell in the shadows.

8 conventionally cooked pancakes, each about 20 cm/8 in diameter
45 ml/3 tbsp butter
30 ml/2 tbsp caster (superfine) sugar
5 ml/1 tsp grated orange peel
5 ml/1 tsp grated lemon peel
Juice of 2 large oranges
30 ml/2 tbsp Grand Marnier
30 ml/2 tbsp brandy

Fold each pancake in four so that it looks like an envelope. Leave aside. Put the butter in a shallow 25 cm/10 in diameter dish. Melt on Defrost for 1½–2 minutes. Add all the remaining ingredients except the brandy and stir well. Heat on Full for 2–2½ minutes. Stir round. Add the pancakes in a single layer and baste with the butter sauce. Cook, uncovered, on Full for 3–4 minutes. Remove from the microwave. Pour the brandy into a cup and heat on Full for 15–20 seconds until tepid. Tip into a ladle and ignite with a match. Pour over the crêpes and serve when the flames have died down.

Baked Apples

For 1 apple: score a line round a large cooking (tart) apple with a sharp knife, about one-third down from the top. Remove the core with a potato peeler or apple corer, taking care not to cut through the base of the apple. Fill with sugar, dried fruit, jam (conserve) or lemon curd. Place in a dish and cook, uncovered, on Full for 3–4 minutes, turning the dish twice, until the apple has puffed up like a soufflé. Allow to stand for 2 minutes before eating.

For 2 apples: as for 1 apple, but arrange the apples side by side on the dish and cook on Full for 5 minutes.

For 3 apples: as for 1 apple, but arrange in a triangle in the dish and cook on Full for 7 minutes.

For 4 apples: as for 1 apple, but arrange in a square in the dish and cook on Full for 8–10 minutes.

Braised Beef and Vegetables

Serves 4

30 ml/2 tbsp butter or margarine, at kitchen temperature
1 large onion, grated
3 carrots, thinly sliced
75 g/3 oz mushrooms, thinly sliced
450 g/1 lb rump (tip) steak, cut into small cubes
1 beef stock cube
15 ml/1 tbsp plain (all-purpose) flour
300 ml/½ pt/1¼ cups hot water or beef stock
Freshly ground black pepper
5 ml/1 tsp salt

Put the butter or margarine into a 20 cm/8 in diameter casserole dish (Dutch oven). Melt on Defrost for 45 seconds. Add the vegetables and steak and mix well. Cook, uncovered, on Full for 3 minutes. Crumble in the stock cube and stir in the flour and hot water or stock. Move the mixture to the edge of the dish to form a ring, leaving a small hollow in the centre. Sprinkle with pepper. Cover with clingfilm (plastic wrap) and slit it twice to allow steam to escape. Cook on Full for 9 minutes, turning the dish once. Allow to stand for 5 minutes, then season with the salt and serve.

Beef Stew

Serves 4

450 g/1 lb lean stewing steak, cut into small cubes
15 ml/1 tbsp plain (all-purpose) flour
250 g/9 oz unthawed frozen vegetable stewpack
300 ml/½ pt/1¼ cups boiling water
1 beef stock cube
Freshly ground pepper
2.5–5 ml/½–1 tsp salt

Put the steak in a 23 cm/9 in diameter casserole dish (Dutch oven), not too deep. Sprinkle with the flour, then toss well to coat. Spread out loosely into a single layer. Break up the vegetables, then arrange round the meat. Cover with clingfilm (plastic wrap) and slit it twice to allow steam to escape. Cook on Full for 15 minutes, turning the dish four times. Pour the water over the meat and crumble in the stock cube. Season to taste with pepper and stir thoroughly. Cover as before, then cook on Full for 10 minutes, turning the dish three times. Allow to stand for 5 minutes, then stir round, season with the salt and serve.

Beef and Vegetable Hot-pot

Serves 4

450 g/1 lb potatoes
2 carrots
1 large onion
450 g/1 lb lean stewing steak, cut into small cubes
1 beef stock cube
150 ml/¼ pt/2/3 cup hot beef or vegetable stock
30 ml/2 tbsp butter or margarine

Cut the potatoes, carrots and the onion into transparent wafer-thin slices. Separate the onion slices into rings. Thoroughly grease a 1.75 litre/3 pt/7½ cup dish. Fill with alternate layers of the vegetables and meat, beginning and ending with the potatoes. Cover with clingfilm (plastic wrap) and slit it twice to allow steam to escape. Cook on Full for 15 minutes, turning the dish three times. Crumble the stock cube into the hot stock and stir until dissolved. Pour gently down the side of the dish so it flows through the meat and vegetables. Top with flakes of the butter or margarine. Cover as before and cook on Full for 15 minutes, turning the dish three times. Allow to stand for 5 minutes. Brown under a hot grill (broiler), if liked.

Beef Curry

Serves 4–5

An Anglicised version of a medium-hot curry. Serve with basmati rice and sambals (side dishes) of plain yoghurt, sliced cucumber sprinkled with chopped fresh coriander (cilantro), and chutney.

450 g/1 lb lean stewing beef, cut into small cubes
2 onions, chopped
2 garlic cloves, crushed
15 ml/1 tbsp sunflower or corn oil
30 ml/2 tbsp hot curry powder
30 ml/2 tbsp tomato purée (paste)
15 ml/1 tbsp plain (all-purpose) flour
4 green cardamom pods
15 ml/1 tbsp garam masala
450 ml/¾ pt/2 cups hot water
5 ml/1 tsp salt

Arrange the meat in a single layer in a deep 25 cm/10 in diameter dish. Cover with a plate and cook on Full for 15 minutes, stirring twice. Meanwhile, fry (sauté) the onions and garlic conventionally in the oil in a frying pan (skillet) over a medium heat until pale golden. Stir in the curry powder, tomato purée, flour, cardamom pods and garam masala, then gradually blend in the hot water. Cook, stirring, until the mixture comes to the boil and thickens. Remove the dish of meat from the microwave and stir in the contents of the frying pan. Cover with clingfilm (plastic wrap) and slit it twice to allow steam to escape. Cook on Full for 10 minutes, turning the dish twice. Allow to stand for 5 minutes before serving.

Basic Mince

Serves 4

450 g/1 lb/4 cups lean minced (ground) beef
1 onion, grated
30 ml/2 tbsp plain (all-purpose) flour
450 ml/¾ pt/2 cups hot water
1 beef stock cube
5 ml/1 tsp salt

Place the meat in a deep 20 cm/8 in diameter dish. Thoroughly mix in the onion and flour with a fork. Cook, uncovered, on Full for 5 minutes. Break up the meat with a fork. Add the water and crumble in the stock cube. Stir well to mix. Cover with clingfilm (plastic wrap) and slit it twice to allow steam to escape. Cook on Full for 15 minutes, turning the dish four times. Allow to stand for 4 minutes. Add the salt and stir round before serving.

Cottage Pie

Serves 4

1 quantity Basic Mince
675 g/1½ lb freshly cooked potatoes
30 ml/2 tbsp butter or margarine
60–90 ml/4–6 tbsp hot milk

Cool the Basic Mince to lukewarm and transfer to a greased 1 litre/1¾ pt/4¼ cup pie dish. Cream the potatoes with the butter or margarine and enough of the milk to make a light and fluffy mash. Pipe over the meat mixture or spread smoothly then rough up with a fork. Reheat, uncovered, on Full for 3 minutes. Alternatively, brown under a hot grill (broiler).

Cottage Pie with Cheese

Serves 4

Prepare as for Cottage Pie, but add 50–75 g/2–3 oz/½–¾ cup grated Cheddar cheese to the potatoes after creaming with the butter and hot milk.

Mince with Oats

Serves 4

Prepare as for Basic Mince, but add 1 carrot, grated, with the onion. Substitute 25 g/1 oz/½ cup porridge oats for the flour. Cook for the first time for 7 minutes.

Chilli con Carne

Serves 4–5

450 g/1 lb/4 cups lean minced (ground) beef
1 onion, grated
2 garlic cloves, crushed
5–20 ml/1–4 tsp chilli seasoning
400 g/14 oz/1 large can chopped tomatoes
5 ml/1 tsp Worcestershire sauce
400 g/14 oz/1 large can red kidney beans, drained
5 ml/1 tsp salt
Jacket Potatoes or boiled rice, to serve

Put the beef into a 23 cm/9 in diameter casserole dish (Dutch oven). Stir in the onion and garlic with a fork. Cook, uncovered, on Full for 5 minutes. Break up the meat with a fork. Work in all the remaining ingredients except the salt. Cover with clingfilm (plastic wrap) and slit it twice to allow steam to escape. Cook on Full for 15 minutes, turning the dish three times. Allow to stand for 4 minutes. Season with the salt before serving with jacket potatoes or boiled rice.

Curried Mince

Serves 4

2 onions, grated
2 garlic cloves, crushed
450 g/1 lb/4 cups lean minced (ground) beef
15 ml/1 tbsp plain (all-purpose) flour
5–10 ml/1–2 tbsp mild curry powder
30 ml/2 tbsp fruity chutney
60 ml/4 tbsp tomato purée (paste)
300 ml/½ pt/1¼ cups boiling water
1 beef stock cube
Salt and freshly ground black pepper

Mash together the onions, garlic and beef. Spread into a 20 cm/8 in diameter casserole dish (Dutch oven). Form into a ring round the edge of the dish, leaving small hollow in the centre. Cover with plate and cook on Full for 5 minutes. Break up with fork. Work in the flour, curry powder, chutney and tomato purée. Gradually stir in the water, then crumble in the stock cube. Cover with clingfilm (plastic wrap) and slit it twice to allow steam to escape. Cook on Full for 15 minutes, turning the dish three times. Allow to stand for 4 minutes. Season to taste, then stir round and serve.

Beef Goulash

Serves 6

40 g/1½ oz/3 tbsp butter, margarine or lard
675 g/1½ lb stewing steak, cut into small cubes
2 large onions, grated
1 medium green (bell) pepper, seeded and finely diced
2 garlic cloves, crushed
4 tomatoes, blanched, skinned and chopped
45 ml/3 tbsp tomato purée (paste)
15 ml/1 tbsp paprika
5 ml/1 tsp caraway seeds
5 ml/1 tsp salt
300 ml/½ pt/1¼ cups boiling water
150 ml/¼ pt/2/3 cup soured (dairy sour) cream

Put the fat in a 1.75 litre/3 pt/7½ cup dish. Melt, uncovered, on Full for 1 minute. Mix in the meat, onions, peppers and garlic. Cover with clingfilm (plastic wrap) and slit it twice to allow steam to escape. Cook on Full for 15 minutes, turning the dish four times. Uncover and stir in the tomatoes, tomato purée, paprika and caraway seeds. Cover as before and cook on Full for 15 minutes, turning the dish four times. Season with the salt and gently mix in the boiling water. Ladle into deep plates and top each generously with the cream.

Beef Goulash with Boiled Potatoes

Serves 6

Prepare as for Beef Goulash, but omit the cream and add 2–3 whole boiled potatoes to each serving.

Butter Bean and Beef Stew with Tomatoes

Serves 6

425 g/15 oz/1 large can butter beans
275 g/10 oz/1 can tomato soup
30 ml/2 tbsp dried onions
6 slices braising steak, about 125 g/4 oz each, beaten flat
Salt and freshly ground black pepper

Combine the beans, soup and onions in a 20 cm/8 in diameter casserole dish (Dutch oven). Cover with a plate and cook on Full for 6 minutes, stirring three times. Arrange the steaks round the edge of the dish. Cover with clingfilm (plastic wrap) and slit it twice to allow steam to escape. Cook on Full for 17 minutes, turning the dish three times. Allow to stand for 5 minutes. Uncover and season to taste before serving.

Beef and Tomato Cake

Serves 2–3

275 g/10 oz/2½ cups minced (ground) beef
30 ml/2 tbsp plain (all-purpose) flour
1 egg
5 ml/1 tsp onion powder
150 ml/¼ pt/2/3 cup tomato juice
5 ml/1 tsp soy sauce
5 ml/1 tsp dried oregano
Boiled pasta, to serve

Thoroughly grease a 900 ml/1½ pt/3¾ cup oval pie dish. Mix the beef with all remaining ingredients and spread smoothly into the dish. Cover with clingfilm (plastic wrap) and slit it twice to allow steam to escape. Cook on Full for 7 minutes, turning the dish twice. Allow to stand for 5 minutes. Cut into two or three portions and serve hot with pasta.

Beef and Mushroom Kebabs

Serves 4

24 fresh or dried bay leaves
½ red (bell) pepper, cut into small squares
½ green (bell) pepper, cut into small squares
750 g/1½ lb grilling (broiling) steak, trimmed and cut into 2.5 cm/1 in cubes
175 g/6 oz button mushrooms
50 g/2 oz/¼ cup butter or margarine, at kitchen temperature
5 ml/1 tsp paprika
5 ml/1 tsp Worcestershire sauce
1 garlic clove, crushed
175 g/6 oz/1½ cups rice, boiled

If using dried bay leaves, place in a small dish, add 90 ml/6 tbsp water and cover with a saucer. Heat on Full for 2 minutes to soften. Put the pepper squares into a dish and just cover with water. Cover with a plate and heat on Full for 1 minute to soften. Drain the peppers and bay leaves. Thread the beef, mushrooms, pepper squares and bay leaves on to twelve 10 cm/4 in wooden skewers. Arrange the kebabs like the spokes of a wheel in a deep 25 cm/10 in diameter dish. Put the butter or margarine, paprika, Worcestershire sauce and garlic in a small dish and heat, uncovered, on Full for 1 minute. Brush over the kebabs. Cook, uncovered, on Full for 8 minutes, turning the dish four times. Carefully turn the kebabs over and brush with the rest of the butter mixture. Cook on Full for a further 4 minutes, turning the dish twice. Arrange on a bed of rice and coat with the juices from the dish. Allow three kebabs per person.

Stuffed Lamb

Serves 4

A slightly Middle Eastern approach here. Serve the lamb with warm pitta bread and a green salad dotted with olives and capers.

4 pieces neck of lamb fillet, about 15 cm/6 in long and 675 g/½ lb each

3 large slices white bread with crusts, cubed

1 onion, cut into 6 wedges

45 ml/3 tbsp toasted pine nuts

30 ml/2 tbsp currants

2.5 ml/½ tsp salt

150 g/5 oz/2/3 cup thick Greek plain yoghurt

Ground cinnamon

8 button mushrooms

15 ml/1 tbsp olive oil

Trim the fat from the lamb. Make a lengthways slit in each piece, taking care not to cut right through the meat. Grind up the bread cubes and onion pieces together in a food processor or blender. Scrape out into a bowl and mix in the pine nuts, currants and salt. Spread equal amounts into the lamb pieces and secure with wooden cocktail sticks (toothpicks). Arrange in a square in a deep 25 cm/10 in diameter dish. Smear with all the yoghurt and dust lightly with cinnamon. Stud randomly with the mushrooms and coat thinly with the oil. Cover with clingfilm (plastic wrap) and slit it twice to allow steam to escape.

Cook on Full for 16 minutes, turning the dish four times. Allow to stand for 5 minutes, then serve.

Minted Lamb Kebabs

Serves 6

900 g/2 lb neck of lamb fillet, trimmed
12 large mint leaves
60 ml/4 tbsp thick plain yoghurt
60 ml/4 tbsp tomato ketchup (catsup)
1 garlic clove, crushed
5 ml/1 tsp Worcestershire sauce
6 pitta breads, warmed
Lettuce leaves, tomato and cucumber slices

Cut the meat into 2.5 cm/1 in cubes. Thread on to six wooden skewers alternately with the mint leaves. Arrange like the spokes of a wheel in a deep 25 cm/10 in diameter dish. Thoroughly combine the yoghurt, ketchup, garlic and Worcestershire sauce and brush half the mixture over the kebabs. Cook, uncovered, on Full for 8 minutes, turning the dish twice. Turn the kebabs over and brush with the remaining baste. Cook on Full for a further 8 minutes, turning the dish twice. Allow to stand for 5 minutes. Warm the pitta breads briefly under the grill (broiler) until they puff up, then slice along the long edge to make a pocket. Remove the meat from the skewers and discard the bay leaves. Pack the lamb into the pittas, then add a good helping of the salad to each.

Classic Lamb Kebabs

Serves 6

900 g/2 lb neck of lamb fillet, trimmed
12 large mint leaves
30 ml/2 tbsp butter or margarine
5 ml/1 tsp garlic salt
5 ml/1 tsp Worcestershire sauce
5 ml/1 tsp soy sauce
2.5 ml/½ tsp paprika
6 pitta breads, warmed
Lettuce leaves, tomato and cucumber slices

Cut the meat into 2.5 cm/1 in cubes. Thread on to six wooden skewers alternately with the mint leaves. Arrange like the spokes of a wheel in a deep 25 cm/10 in diameter dish. Melt the butter or margarine on Full for 1 minute, then add the garlic salt, Worcestershire sauce, soy sauce and paprika and mix together thoroughly. Brush half the mixture over the kebabs. Cook, uncovered, on Full for 8 minutes, turning the dish twice. Turn the kebabs over and brush with the remaining baste. Cook on Full for a further 8 minutes, turning the dish twice. Allow to stand for 5 minutes. Warm the pitta breads briefly under the grill (broiler) until they puff up, then slice along the long edge to make a pocket. Remove the meat from the skewers and discard the bay leaves. Pack the lamb into the pittas, then add a good helping of the salad to each.

Middle Eastern Lamb with Fruit

Serves 4–6

This delicately spiced and fruited lamb dish is understated elegance, enhanced by its coating of toasted pine nuts and flaked almonds. Serve with yoghurt and buttery rice.

675 g/1½ lb boned lamb, as lean as possible
5 ml/1 tsp ground cinnamon
2.5 ml/½ tsp ground cloves
30 ml/2 tbsp light soft brown sugar
1 onion, chopped
30 ml/2 tbsp lemon juice
10 ml/2 tsp cornflour (cornstarch)
15 ml/1 tbsp cold water
7.5–10 ml/1½–2 tsp salt
400 g/14 oz/1 large can peach slices in natural or apple juice, drained
30 ml/2 tbsp toasted pine nuts
30 ml/2 tbsp flaked (slivered) almonds

Cut the lamb into small cubes. Place in a 1.75 litre/3 pt/7½ cup casserole dish (Dutch oven). Mix together the spices, sugar, onion and lemon juice and add to the dish. Cover with a plate and cook on Full for 5 minutes, then allow to stand for 5 minutes. Repeat three times, stirring well each time. Mix together the cornflour and water to make a smooth paste. Drain the liquid from the lamb and add the cornflour mixture and salt. Pour over the lamb and stir well to mix. Cook, uncovered, on Full for 2 minutes. Stir in the peach slices and cook, uncovered, on Full for a further 1½ minutes. Sprinkle with the pine nuts and almonds and and serve.

Mock Irish Stew

Serves 4

675 g/1½ lb cubed stewing lamb
2 large onions, coarsely grated
450 g/1 lb potatoes, finely diced
300 ml/½ pt/1¼ cups boiling water
5 ml/1 tsp salt
45 ml/3 tbsp chopped parsley

Trim away any excess fat from the lamb. Place the meat and vegetables in a single layer in a deep 25 cm/10 in diameter dish. Cover with clingfilm (plastic wrap) and slit it twice to allow steam to escape. Cook on Full for 15 minutes, turning the dish twice. Mix the water and salt and pour over the meat and vegetables, stirring thoroughly to combine. Cover as before and cook on Full for 20 minutes, turning the dish three times. Allow to stand for 10 minutes. Uncover and sprinkle with the parsley before serving.

Farmer's Wife Lamb Chops

Serves 4

3 cold cooked potatoes, thinly sliced
3 cold cooked carrots, thinly sliced
4 lean lamb chops, 150 g/5 oz each
1 small onion, grated
1 cooking (tart) apple, peeled and grated
30 ml/2 tbsp apple juice
Salt and freshly ground black pepper
15 ml/1 tbsp butter or margarine

Arrange the potato and carrot slices in a single layer over the base of a deep 20 cm/8 in diameter dish. Arrange the chops on top. Sprinkle with the onion and apple and pour the juice over. Season to taste and dot with flakes of the butter or margarine. Cover with clingfilm (plastic wrap) and slit it twice to allow steam to escape. Cook on Full for 15 minutes, turning the dish twice. Allow to stand for 5 minutes before serving.

Lamb Hot-pot

Serves 4

675 g/1½ lb potatoes, very thinly sliced
2 onions, very thinly sliced
3 carrots, very thinly sliced
2 large celery stalks, cut diagonally into thin strips
8 best end of neck lamb chops, about 1 kg/2 lb in all
1 beef stock cube
300 ml/½ pt/1¼ cups boiling water
5 ml/1 tsp salt
25 ml/1½ tbsp melted butter or margarine

Arrange half the prepared vegetables in layers in a lightly greased 2.25 litre/4 pt/10 cup casserole dish (Dutch oven). Place the chops on top and cover with the remaining vegetables. Cover with clingfilm (plastic wrap) and slit it twice to allow steam to escape. Cook on Full for 15 minutes, turning the dish three times. Remove from the microwave and uncover. Crumble the stock cube into the water and add the salt. Pour gently down the side of the casserole. Trickle the butter or margarine over the top. Cover as before and cook on Full for 15 minutes. Allow to stand for 6 minutes before serving.

Lamb Loaf with Mint and Rosemary

Serves 4

450 g/1 lb/4 cups minced (ground) lamb
1 garlic clove, crushed
2.5 ml/½ tsp dried crumbled rosemary
2.5 ml/½ tsp dried mint
30 ml/2 tbsp plain (all-purpose) flour
2 large eggs, beaten
2.5 ml/½ tsp salt
5 ml/1 tsp brown table sauce
Grated nutmeg

Lightly grease a 900 ml/1½ pt/3¾ cup oval pie dish. Mix together all the ingredients except the nutmeg and spread smoothly into the dish. Cover with clingfilm (plastic wrap) and slit it twice to allow steam to escape. Cook on Full for 8 minutes, turning the dish twice. Allow to stand for 4 minutes, then uncover and sprinkle with nutmeg. Cut into portions to serve.

Lamb Bredie with Tomatoes

Serves 6

Prepare as for Chicken Bredie with Tomatoes, but substitute boned and coarsely chopped lamb for the chicken.

Lamb Biriani

Serves 4–6

5 cardamom pods
30 ml/2 tbsp sunflower oil
450 g/1 lb trimmed neck of lamb fillet, cut into small cubes
2 garlic cloves, crushed
20 ml/4 tsp garam masala
225 g/8 oz/1¼ cups easy-cook long-grain rice
600 ml/1 pt/2½ cups hot chicken stock
10 ml/2 tsp salt
125 g/4 oz/1 cup flaked (slivered) almonds, toasted

Split the cardamom pods to remove the seeds, then crush the seeds with a pestle and mortar. Heat the oil in a 1.5 litre/3 pt/7½ cup casserole dish (Dutch oven) on Full for 1½ minutes. Add the lamb, garlic, cardamom seeds and garam masala. Mix well, then arrange round the edge of the dish, leaving a small hollow in the centre. Cover with clingfilm (plastic wrap) and slit it twice to allow steam to escape. Cook on Full for 10 minutes. Uncover and mix in the rice, stock and salt. Cover as before and cook on Full for 15 minutes. Allow to stand for 3 minutes, then spoon out on to warmed plates and sprinkle each portion with the almonds.

Ornate Biriani

Serves 4–6

Prepare as for Lamb Biriani, but arrange the biriani on a warmed serving dish and garnish with chopped hard-boiled (hard-cooked) eggs, tomato wedges, coriander (cilantro) leaves and fried (sautéed) chopped onion.

Moussaka

Serves 6–8

You require a little patience to prepare this multi-layered lamb-based Greek classic but the results are well worth the effort. Poached aubergine (eggplant) slices makes this less rich and easier to digest than some versions.

For the aubergine layers:
675 g/1½ lb aubergines
75 ml/5 tbsp hot water
5 ml/1 tsp salt
15 ml/1 tbsp fresh lemon juice

For the meat layers:
40 g/1½ oz/3 tbsp butter, margarine or olive oil
2 onions, finely chopped
1 garlic clove, crushed
350 g/12 oz/3 cups cold cooked minced (ground) lamb
125 g/4 oz/2 cups fresh white breadcrumbs
Salt and freshly ground black pepper
4 tomatoes, blanched, skinned and sliced

For the sauce:
425 ml/¾ pt/scant 2 cups full- cream milk
40 g/1½ oz/3 tbsp butter or margarine
45 ml/3 tbsp plain (all-purpose) flour

75 g/3 oz/¾ cup Cheddar cheese, grated

1 egg yolk

Moussaka with Potatoes

Serves 6–8

Prepare as for Moussaka, but substitute sliced cooked potatoes for the aubergines (eggplants).

Quick Moussaka

Serves 3–4

A quick alternative with an acceptable flavour and texture.

1 aubergine (eggplant), about 225 g/8 oz
15 ml/1 tbsp cold water
300 ml/½ pt/1¼ cups cold milk
300 ml/½ pt/1¼ cups water
1 packet instant mashed potato to serve 4
225 g/8 oz/2 cups cold cooked minced (ground) lamb
5 ml/1 tsp dried marjoram
5 ml/1 tsp salt
2 garlic cloves, crushed
3 tomatoes, blanched, skinned and sliced
150 ml/¼ pt/2/3 cup thick Greek plain yoghurt
1 egg
Salt and freshly ground black pepper
50 g/2 oz/½ cup Cheddar cheese, grated

Top and tail the aubergine and halve it lengthways. Place in a shallow dish, cut sides uppermost and sprinkle with the cold water. Cover with clingfilm (plastic wrap) and slit it twice to allow steam to escape. Cook on Full for 5½–6 minutes until tender. Allow to stand for 2 minutes, then drain. Pour the milk and water into a bowl and stir in the dried potato. Cover with a plate and cook on Full for 6 minutes. Stir well, then mix in the lamb, marjoram, salt and garlic. Slice the unpeeled aubergine. Arrange alternate layers of aubergine slices and the potato mixture in a 2.25 litre/4 pt/10 cup greased casserole dish (Dutch oven), using half the tomato slices to form a 'sandwich filling' in the centre. Cover with the remaining tomato slices. Beat together the yoghurt and egg and season to taste. Spoon over the tomatoes and sprinkle with the cheese. Cover with clingfilm as before. Cook on Full for 7 minutes. Uncover and brown under a hot grill (broiler) before serving.

Lamb Mince

Serves 4

Prepare as for Basic Mince, but substitute minced (ground) lamb for the minced beef.

Shepherd's Pie

Serves 4

Prepare as for Basic Mince, but substitute lamb mince for beef. Cool to lukewarm, then transfer to a 1 litre/1¾ pt/4½ cup greased pie dish. Top with 750 g/1½ lb hot mashed potato creamed with 15–30 ml/1–2 tbsp butter or margarine and 60 ml/4 tbsp hot milk. Season well with salt and freshly ground black pepper. Spread over the meat mixture, then rough up with a fork. Reheat, uncovered, on Full for 2–3 minutes or brown under a hot grill (broiler).

Country Liver in Red Wine

Serves 4

25 g/1 oz/2 tbsp butter or margarine
2 onions, grated
450 g/1 lb lambs' liver, cut into narrow strips
15 ml/1 tbsp plain (all-purpose) flour
300 ml/½ pt/1¼ cups red wine
15 ml/1 tbsp dark soft brown sugar
1 beef stock cube, crumbled
30 ml/2 tbsp chopped parsley
Salt and freshly ground black pepper
Buttered boiled potatoes and lightly cooked shredded cabbage, to serve

Put the butter or margarine in a deep 25 cm/10 in diameter dish. Melt, uncovered, on Defrost for 2 minutes. Stir in the onions and liver. Cover with a plate and cook on Full for 5 minutes. Mix in all the remaining ingredients except the salt and pepper. Cover with a plate and cook on Full for 6 minutes, stirring twice. Allow to stand for 3 minutes. Season to taste and serve with buttered boiled potatoes and cabbage.

Liver and Bacon

Serves 4–6

2 onions, grated
8 bacon rashers (slices), coarsely chopped
450 g/1 lb lambs' liver, cut into small cubes
45 ml/3 tbsp cornflour (cornstarch)
60 ml/4 tbsp cold water
150 ml/¼ pt/2/3 cup boiling water
Salt and freshly ground black pepper

Put the onions and bacon in a 1.75 litre/3 pt/7½ cup casserole dish (Dutch oven). Cook, uncovered, on Full for 7 minutes, stirring twice. Mix in the liver. Cover with a plate and cook on Full for 8 minutes, stirring three times. Mix the cornflour with the cold water to make a smooth paste. Stir into the liver and onions, then gradually blend in the boiling water. Cover with a plate and cook on Full for 6 minutes, stirring three times. Allow to stand for 4 minutes. Season to taste and serve.

Liver and Bacon with Apple

Serves 4–6

Prepare as for Liver and Bacon, but substitute 1 eating (dessert) apple, peeled and grated, for one of the onions. Substitute apple juice at room temperature for half the boiling water.

Kidneys in Red Wine with Brandy

Serves 4

6 lambs' kidneys
30 ml/2 tbsp butter or margarine
1 onion, finely chopped
30 ml/2 tbsp plain (all-purpose) flour
150 ml/¼ pt/2/3 cup dry red wine
2 beef stock cubes
50 g/2 oz mushrooms, sliced
10 ml/2 tsp tomato purée (paste)
2.5 ml/½ tsp paprika
2.5 ml/½ tsp mustard powder
30 ml/2 tbsp chopped parsley
30 ml/2 tbsp brandy

Skin and halve the kidneys, then cut out and discard the cores with a sharp knife. Slice very thinly. Melt half the butter, uncovered, on Defrost for 1 minute. Stir in the kidneys and set aside. Put the remaining butter and the onion in a 1.5 litre/2½ pt/6 cup dish. Cook, uncovered, on Full for 2 minutes, stirring once. Mix in the flour, then the wine. Cook, uncovered, on Full for 3 minutes, stirring briskly every minute. Crumble in the stock cubes, then stir in the mushrooms, tomato purée, paprika, mustard and the kidneys with the butter or margarine. Mix thoroughly. Cover with clingfilm (plastic wrap) and slit it twice to allow steam to escape. Cook on Full for 5 minutes, turning the dish once. Allow to stand for 3 minutes, then uncover and sprinkle with the parsley. Warm the brandy in a cup on Full for 10–15 seconds. Pour over the kidney mixture and ignite. Serve when the flames have subsided.

Venison Steaks with Oyster Mushrooms and Blue Cheese

Serves 4

Salt and freshly ground black pepper
8 small venison steaks
5 ml/1 tsp juniper berries, crushed
5 ml/1 tsp herbes de Provence
30 ml/2 tbsp olive oil
300 ml/½ pt/1¼ cups dry red wine
60 ml/4 tbsp rich beef stock
60 ml/4 tbsp gin
1 onion, chopped
225 g/8 oz oyster mushrooms, trimmed and sliced
250 ml/8 fl oz/1 cup single (light) cream
30 ml/2 tbsp redcurrant jelly (clear conserve)
60 ml/4 tbsp blue cheese, crumbled
30 ml/2 tbsp chopped parsley

Season the venison to taste, then work in the juniper berries and herbes de Provence. Heat the oil in a browning dish on Full for 2 minutes. Add the steaks and cook, uncovered, on Full for 3 minutes, turning once. Add the wine, stock, gin, onion, mushrooms, cream and redcurrant jelly. Cover with clingfilm (plastic wrap) and slit it twice to allow steam to escape. Cook on Medium for 25 minutes, turning the dish four times. Mix in the cheese. Cover with a heatproof plate and cook on Full for 2 minutes. Allow to stand for 3 minutes, then uncover and serve garnished with the parsley.

Cooking Small Pasta

Follow the directions for cooking large pasta but cook for only 4–5 minutes. Cover and stand for 3 minutes, then drain and serve.

Chinese Noodle and Mushroom Salad with Walnuts

Serves 6

30 ml/2 tbsp sesame oil
175 g/6 oz mushrooms, sliced
250 g/9 oz thread egg noodles
7.5 ml/1½ tsp salt
75 g/3 oz/¾ cup chopped walnuts
5 spring onions (scallions), chopped
30 ml/2 tbsp soy sauce

Heat the oil, uncovered, on Defrost for 2½ minutes. Add the mushrooms. Cover with a plate and cook on Full for 3 minutes, stirring twice. Set aside. Put the noodles in a large bowl and add enough boiling water to come 5 cm/2 in above the level of the pasta. Stir in the salt. Cook, uncovered, on Full for 4–5 minutes until the noodles swell and are just tender. Drain and allow to cool. Mix in the remaining ingredients including the mushrooms and toss well to mix.

Pepper Macaroni

Serves 2

300 ml/½ pt/1¼ cups tomato juice
125 g/4 oz/1 cup elbow macaroni
5 ml/1 tsp salt
30 ml/2 tbsp white wine, heated
1 small red or green (bell) pepper, seeded and chopped
45 ml/3 tbsp olive oil
75 g/3 oz/¾ cup Gruyère (Swiss) or Emmental cheese, grated
30 ml/2 tbsp chopped parsley

Pour the tomato juice into a 1.25 litre/2¼ pt/5½ cup dish. Cover with a plate and heat on Full for 3½–4 minutes until very hot and bubbling. Stir in all the remaining ingredients except the cheese and parsley. Cover as before and cook on Full for 10 minutes, stirring twice. Allow to stand for 5 minutes. Sprinkle with the cheese and parsley. Reheat, uncovered, on Full for about 1 minute until the cheese melts.

Family Macaroni Cheese

Serves 6–7

For convenience, this recipe is for a large family-sized meal, but any leftovers can be reheated in portions in the microwave.

350 g/12 oz/3 cups elbow macaroni
10 ml/2 tsp salt
30 ml/2 tbsp cornflour (cornstarch)
600 ml/1 pt/2½ cups cold milk
1 egg, beaten
10 ml/2 tsp made mustard
Freshly ground black pepper
275 g/10 oz/2½ cups Cheddar cheese, grated

Put the macaroni in a deep dish. Stir in the salt and sufficient boiling water to come 5 cm/2 in above the level of the pasta. Cook, uncovered, on Full for about 10 minutes until just tender, stirring three times. Drain if necessary, then leave to stand while preparing the sauce. In a separate large bowl, mix the cornflour smoothly with some of the cold milk, then mix in the remainder. Cook, uncovered, on Full for 6–7 minutes until smoothly thickened, whisking every minute. Mix in the egg, mustard and pepper followed by two-thirds of the cheese and all the macaroni. Mix thoroughly with a fork. Spread evenly into a buttered 30 cm/12 in diameter dish. Sprinkle the remaining cheese over the top. Reheat, uncovered, on Full for 4–5 minutes. If liked, brown quickly under a hot grill (broiler) before serving.

Classic Macaroni Cheese

Serves 4–5

This version is slightly richer than Family Macaroni Cheese and lends itself to a number of variations.

225 g/8 oz/2 cups elbow macaroni
7.5 ml/1½ tsp salt
30 ml/2 tbsp butter or margarine
30 ml/2 tbsp plain (all-purpose) flour
300 ml/½ pt/1¼ cups milk
225 g/8 oz/2 cups Cheddar cheese, grated
5–10 ml/1–2 tsp made mustard
Salt and freshly ground black pepper

Put the macaroni in a deep dish. Stir in the salt and sufficient boiling water to come 5 cm/2 in above the level of the pasta. Cook, uncovered, on Full for 8–10 minutes until just tender, stirring two or three times. Stand for 3–4 minutes inside the microwave. Drain if necessary, then leave to stand while preparing the sauce. Melt the butter or margarine, uncovered, on Defrost for 1–1½ minutes. Stir in the flour, then gradually blend in the milk. Cook, uncovered, on Full for 6–7 minutes until smoothly thickened, whisking every minute. Mix in two-thirds of the cheese, followed by the mustard and seasoning, then the macaroni. Spread evenly in a 20 cm/8 in diameter dish. Sprinkle with the remaining cheese. Reheat, uncovered, on Full for 3–4 minutes. If liked, brown quickly under a hot grill (broiler) before serving.

Macaroni Cheese with Stilton

Serves 4–5

Prepare as for Classic Macaroni Cheese, but substitute 100 g/3½ oz/1 cup crumbled Stilton for half the Cheddar cheese.

Macaroni Cheese with Bacon

Serves 4–5

Prepare as for Classic Macaroni Cheese, but stir in 6 rashers (slices) streaky bacon, grilled (broiled) until crisp then crumbled, with the mustard and seasoning.

Macaroni Cheese with Tomatoes

Serves 4–5

Prepare as for Classic Macaroni Cheese, but place a layer of tomato slices from about 3 skinned tomatoes on top of the pasta before sprinkling with the remaining cheese.

Spaghetti Carbonara

Serves 4

75 ml/5 tbsp double (heavy) cream
2 large eggs
100 g/4 oz/1 cup Parma ham, chopped
175 g/6 oz/1½ cups grated Parmesan cheese
350 g/12 oz spaghetti or other large pasta

Beat together the cream and eggs. Stir in the ham and 90 ml/6 tbsp of the Parmesan. Cook the spaghetti as directed. Drain and place in a serving dish. Add the cream mixture and toss all together with two wooden forks or spoons. Cover with kitchen paper and reheat on Full for 1½ minutes. Serve each portion topped with the remaining Parmesan.

Pizza-style Macaroni Cheese

Serves 4–5

225 g/8 oz/2 cups elbow macaroni
7.5 ml/1½ tsp salt
30 ml/2 tbsp butter or margarine
30 ml/2 tbsp plain (all-purpose) flour
300 ml/½ pt/1¼ cups milk
125 g/4 oz/1 cup Cheddar cheese, grated
125 g/4 oz/1 cup Mozzarella cheese, grated
5–10 ml/1–2 tsp made mustard
Salt and freshly ground black pepper
212 g/7 oz/1 small can tuna in oil, drained and oil reserved
12 stoned (pitted) black olives, sliced
1 canned pimiento, sliced
2 tomatoes, blanched, skinned and coarsely chopped
5–10 ml/1–2 tsp red or green pesto (optional)
Basil leaves, to garnish

Put the macaroni in a deep dish. Stir in the salt and sufficient boiling water to come 5 cm/2 in above the level of the pasta. Cook, uncovered, on Full for 8–10 minutes until just tender, stirring two or three times. Stand for 3–4 minutes inside the microwave. Drain if necessary, then leave to stand while preparing the sauce. Melt the butter or margarine, uncovered, on Defrost for 1–1½ minutes. Stir in the flour, then gradually blend in the milk. Cook, uncovered, on Full for 6–7 minutes until smoothly thickened, whisking every minute. Mix in two-thirds of each cheese, followed by the mustard and seasoning. Stir in the macaroni, tuna, 15 ml/1 tbsp of the tuna oil, the olives, pimiento, tomatoes and pesto, if using. Spread evenly in a 20 cm/8 in diameter dish. Sprinkle with the remaining cheeses. Reheat, uncovered, on Full for 3–4 minutes. If liked, brown quickly under a hot grill (broiler) before serving garnished with basil leaves.

Spaghetti Cream with Spring Onions

Serves 4

150 ml/¼ pt/2/3 cup double (heavy) cream
1 egg yolk
150 g/5 oz/1¼ cups grated Parmesan cheese
8 spring onions (scallions), finely chopped
Salt and freshly ground black pepper
350 g/12 oz spaghetti or other large pasta

Beat together the cream, egg yolk, 45 ml/3 tbsp of the Parmesan and the spring onions. Season well to taste. Cook the spaghetti as directed. Drain and place in a serving dish. Add the cream mixture and toss all together with two wooden forks or spoons. Cover with kitchen paper and reheat on Full for 1½ minutes. Offer the remaining Parmesan cheese separately.

Spaghetti Bolognese

Serves 4–6

450 g/1 lb/4 cups lean minced (ground) beef
1 garlic clove, crushed
1 large onion, grated
1 green (bell) pepper, seeded and finely chopped
5 ml/1 tsp Italian seasoning or dried mixed herbs
400 g/14 oz/1 large can chopped tomatoes
45 ml/3 tbsp tomato purée (paste)
1 beef stock cube
75 ml/5 tbsp red wine or water
15 ml/1 tbsp dark soft brown sugar
5 ml/1 tsp salt
Freshly ground black pepper
350 g/12 oz freshly cooked and drained spaghetti or other pasta
Grated Parmesan cheese

Combine the beef with the garlic in a 1.75 litre/3 pt/7½ cup dish. Cook, uncovered, on Full for 5 minutes. Mix in all the remaining ingredients except the salt, pepper and spaghetti. Cover with a plate and cook on Full for 15 minutes, stirring four times with a fork to break up the meat. Allow to stand for 4 minutes. Season with the salt and pepper to taste and serve with the spaghetti. Offer the Parmesan cheese separately.

Spaghetti with Turkey Bolognese Sauce

Serves 4

Prepare as for Spaghetti Bolognese, but substitute minced (ground) turkey for the beef.

Spaghetti with Ragu Sauce

Serves 4

A traditional and economical sauce, first used in England in Soho trattorias shortly after World War Two.

20 ml/4 tsp olive oil
1 large onion, finely chopped
1 garlic clove, crushed
1 small carrot, grated
250 g/8 oz/2 cups lean minced (ground) beef
10 ml/2 tsp plain (all-purpose) flour
15 ml/1 tbsp tomato purée (paste)
300 ml/½ pt/1¼ cups beef stock
45 ml/3 tbsp dry white wine
1.5 ml/¼ tsp dried basil
1 small bay leaf
175 g/6 oz mushrooms, coarsely chopped
Salt and freshly ground black pepper
350 g/12 oz freshly cooked and drained spaghetti or other pasta
Grated Parmesan cheese

Place the oil, onion, garlic and carrot in a 1.75 litre/3 pt/7½ cup dish. Heat, uncovered, on Full for 6 minutes. Add all the remaining ingredients except the salt, pepper and spaghetti. Cover with a plate and cook on Full for 11 minutes, stirring three times. Allow to stand for 4 minutes. Season with salt and pepper, remove the bay leaf and serve with the spaghetti. Offer the Parmesan cheese separately.

Spaghetti with Butter

Serves 4

350 g/12 oz pasta
60 ml/4 tbsp butter or olive oil
Grated Parmesan cheese

Cook the pasta as directed. Drain and place in a large dish with the butter or olive oil. Toss with two spoons until the pasta is well coated. Spoon on to four warmed plates and heap grated Parmesan cheese on each.

Pasta with Garlic

Serves 4

350 g/12 oz pasta
2 cloves garlic, crushed
50 g/2 oz butter
10 ml/2 tsp olive oil
30 ml/2 tbsp chopped parsley
Grated Parmesan cheese
Rocket or radicchio leaves, shredded

Cook the pasta as directed. Heat the garlic, butter and oil on Full for 1½ minutes. Stir in the parsley. Drain the pasta and place in a serving dish. Add the garlic mixture and toss all together with two wooden spoons. Serve straight away sprinkled with Parmesan and garnished with shredded rocket or radicchio leaves.

Spaghetti with Beef and Mixed Vegetable Bolognese Sauce

Serves 4

30 ml/2 tbsp olive oil
1 large onion, finely chopped
2 garlic cloves, crushed
4 rashers (slices) streaky bacon, chopped
1 celery stalk, chopped
1 carrot, grated
125 g/4 oz button mushrooms, thinly sliced
225 g/8 oz/2 cups lean minced (ground) beef
30 ml/2 tbsp plain (all-purpose) flour
1 wine glass dry red wine
150 ml/¼ pt/2/3 cup passata (sieved tomatoes)
60 ml/4 tbsp beef stock
2 large tomatoes, blanched, skinned and chopped
15 ml/1 tbsp dark soft brown sugar
1.5 ml/¼ tsp grated nutmeg
15 ml/1 tbsp chopped basil leaves
Salt and freshly ground black pepper
350 g/12 oz freshly cooked and drained spaghetti
Grated Parmesan cheese

Put the oil, onion, garlic, bacon, celery and carrot in a 2 litre/3½ pt/8½ cup dish. Add the mushrooms and meat. Cook, uncovered, on Full for 6 minutes, stirring twice with a fork to break up the meat. Mix in all the remaining ingredients except the salt, pepper and spaghetti. Cover with a plate and cook on Full for 13–15 minutes, stirring three times. Allow to stand for 4 minutes. Season with salt and pepper and serve with the pasta. Offer the Parmesan cheese separately.

Spaghetti with Meat Sauce and Cream

Serves 4

Prepare as for Spaghetti with Beef and Mixed Vegetable Bolognese Sauce, but stir in 30–45 ml/2–3 tbsp double (heavy) cream at the end.

Spaghetti with Marsala Meat Sauce

Serves 4

Prepare as for Spaghetti with Beef and Mixed Vegetable Bolognese Sauce, but substitute marsala for the wine and add 45 ml/3 tbsp Marscapone cheese at the end.

Pasta alla Marinara

Serves 4

This means 'sailor style' and comes from Naples.
30 ml/2 tbsp olive oil
3–4 garlic cloves, crushed
8 large tomatoes, blanched, skinned and chopped
5 ml/1 tsp finely chopped mint
15 ml/1 tbsp finely chopped basil leaves
Salt and freshly ground black pepper
350 g/12 oz freshly cooked and drained pasta
Grated Pecorino or Parmesan cheese, to serve

Put all the ingredients except the pasta in a 1.25 litre/2¼ pt/5½ cup dish. Cover with a plate and cook on Full for 6–7 minutes, stirring three times. Serve with the pasta and offer the Pecorino or Parmesan cheese separately.

Pasta Matriciana

Serves 4

A rustic pasta sauce from the central Abruzzo region in Italy.

30 ml/2 tbsp olive oil
1 onion, chopped
5 rashers (slices) unsmoked streaky bacon, coarsely chopped
8 tomatoes, blanched, skinned and chopped
2–3 garlic cloves, crushed
350 g/12 oz freshly cooked and drained pasta
Grated Pecorino or Parmesan cheese, to serve

Put all the ingredients except the pasta in a 1.25 litre/2¼ pt/5½ cup dish. Cover with a plate and cook on Full for 6 minutes, stirring twice. Serve with the pasta and offer the Pecorino or Parmesan cheese separately.

Pasta with Tuna and Capers

Serves 4

15 ml/1 tbsp butter
200 g/7 oz/1 small can tuna in oil
60 ml/4 tbsp vegetable stock or white wine
15 ml/1 tbsp capers, chopped
30 ml/2 tbsp chopped parsley
350 g/12 oz freshly cooked and drained pasta
Grated Parmesan cheese

Put the butter in a 600 ml/1 pt/2½ cup dish and melt, uncovered, on Defrost for 1½ minutes. Add the contents of the can of tuna and flake the fish. Stir in the stock or wine, capers and parsley. Cover with a plate and heat on Full for 3–4 minutes. Serve with the pasta and offer the Parmesan cheese separately.

Pasta Napoletana

Serves 4

This flamboyant tomato sauce from Naples, with a warm and colourful flavour, is best made in summer when tomatoes are at their most abundant.

8 large ripe tomatoes, blanched, skinned and coarsely chopped
30 ml/2 tbsp olive oil
1 onion, chopped
2–4 garlic cloves, crushed
1 celery stalk, finely chopped
15 ml/1 tbsp chopped basil leaves
10 ml/2 tsp light soft brown sugar
60 ml/4 tbsp water or red wine
Salt and freshly ground black pepper
30 ml/2 tbsp chopped parsley
350 g/12 oz freshly cooked and drained pasta
Grated Parmesan cheese

Put the tomatoes, oil, onion, garlic, celery, basil, sugar and water or wine in a 1.25 litre/2¼ pt/5½ cup dish. Mix well. Cover with a plate and cook on Full for 7 minutes, stirring twice. Season to taste, then stir in the parsley. Serve straight away with the pasta and offer the Parmesan cheese separately.

Pasta Pizzaiola

Serves 4

Prepare as for Pasta Napoletana, but increase the tomatoes to 10, omit the onion, celery and water and use double the amount of parsley. Add 15 ml/1 tbsp fresh or 2.5 ml/½ tsp dried oregano with the parsley.

Pasta with Peas

Serves 4

Prepare as for Pasta Napoletana, but add 125 g/4 oz/1 cup coarsely chopped ham and 175 g/6 oz/1½ cups fresh peas to the tomatoes with the other ingredients. Cook for 9–10 minutes.

Pasta with Chicken Liver Sauce

Serves 4

225 g/8 oz chicken livers
30 ml/2 tbsp plain (all-purpose) flour
15 ml/1 tbsp butter
15 ml/1 tbsp olive oil
1–2 garlic cloves, crushed
125 g/4 oz mushrooms, sliced
150 ml/¼ pt/2/3 cup hot water
150 ml/¼ pt/2/3 cup dry red wine
Salt and freshly ground black pepper
350 g/12 oz pasta, freshly cooked and drained

Pasta with Anchovies

Serves 4

30 ml/2 tbsp olive oil
15 ml/1 tbsp butter
2 garlic cloves, crushed
50 g/2 oz/1 small can anchovy fillets in oil
45 ml/3 tbsp chopped parsley
2.5 ml/½ tsp dried basil
Freshly ground black pepper
350 g/12 oz freshly cooked and drained pasta

Put the oil, butter and garlic in a 600 ml/1 pt/2½ cup dish. Chop the anchovies and add with the oil from the can. Mix in the parsley, basil and pepper to taste. Cover with a plate and cook on Full for 3–3½ minutes. Serve straight away with the pasta.

Ravioli with Sauce

Serves 4

350 g/12 oz/3 cups ravioli

Cook as for large pasta, then serve with any of the tomato-based pasta sauces above.

Tortellini

Serves 4

Allow about 250 g/9 oz bought tortellini and cook as for large fresh or dried pasta. Drain thoroughly, add 25 g/1 oz/2 tbsp unsalted (sweet) butter and toss thoroughly. Serve each portion dusted with grated Parmesan cheese.

Lasagne

Serves 4–6

45 ml/3 tbsp hot water
Spaghetti Bolognese sauce
9–10 sheets no-need-to-precook plain, green (verdi) or brown (wholewheat) lasagne
Cheese Sauce
25 g/1 oz/¼ cup grated Parmesan cheese
30 ml/2 tbsp butter
Grated nutmeg

Oil or butter a 20 cm/8 in square dish. Add the hot water to the Bolognese sauce. Place a layer of lasagne sheets in the bottom of the dish, then a layer of Bolognese sauce, then a layer of cheese sauce. Continue with the layers, finishing with the cheese sauce. Sprinkle with the Parmesan cheese, dot with the butter and dust with nutmeg. Cook, uncovered, for 15 minutes, turning the dish twice. Allow to stand for 5 minutes, then continue to cook for a further 15 minutes or until the lasagne feels soft when a knife is pushed through the centre. (The cooking time will vary depending on the initial temperature of the two sauces.)

Pizza Napoletana

Makes 4

The microwave does a great job on pizzas, reminiscent of the ones you can find all over Italy and in Naples in particular.

30 ml/2 tbsp olive oil
2 onions, peeled and finely chopped
1 garlic clove, crushed
150 g/5 oz/2/3 cup tomato purée (paste)
Basic White or Brown Bread Dough
350 g/12 oz/3 cups Mozzarella cheese, grated
10 ml/2 tsp dried oregano
50 g/2 oz/1 small can anchovy fillets in oil

Cook the oil, onions and garlic, uncovered, on Full for 5 minutes, stirring twice. Mix in the tomato purée and set aside. Divide the dough equally into four pieces. Roll each into a round large enough to cover an oiled and floured 20 cm/8 in flat plate. Cover with kitchen paper and leave to stand for 30 minutes. Spread each with the tomato mixture. Mix the cheese with the oregano and sprinkle equally over each pizza. Garnish with the anchovies. Bake individually, covered with kitchen paper, on Full for 5 minutes, turning twice. Eat straight away.

Pizza Margherita

Makes 4

Prepare as for Pizza Napoletana, but substitute dried basil for the oregano and omit the anchovies.

Seafood Pizza

Makes 4

Prepare as for Pizza Napoletana. When cooked, stud with prawns (shrimp), mussels, clams etc.

Pizza Siciliana

Makes 4

Prepare as for Pizza Napoletana. When cooked, stud with 18 small black olives between the anchovies.

Mushroom Pizza

Makes 4

Prepare as for Pizza Napoletana, but sprinkle 100 g/3½ oz thinly sliced mushrooms over the tomato mixture before adding the cheese and herbs. Cook for an extra 30 seconds.

Ham and Pineapple Pizza

Makes 4

Prepare as for Pizza Napoletana, but sprinkle 125 g/4 oz/1 cup chopped ham over the tomato mixture before adding the cheese and herbs. Chop 2 canned pineapple rings and scatter over the top of the pizza. Cook for an extra 45 seconds.

Pepperoni Pizzas

Makes 4

Prepare as for Pizza Napoletana, but top each pizza with 6 thin slices of pepperoni sausage.

Buttered Flaked Almonds

A splendid topping for sweet and savoury dishes.

15 ml/1 tbsp unsalted (sweet) butter
50 g/2 oz/½ cup flaked (slivered) almonds
Plain or flavoured salt or caster (superfine) sugar

Put the butter in a shallow 20 cm/8 in diameter dish. Melt, uncovered, on Full for 45–60 seconds. Add the almonds and cook, uncovered, on Full for 5–6 minutes until golden brown, stirring and turning every minute. Sprinkle with salt for topping savoury dishes, caster sugar for sweet.

Flaked Almonds in Garlic Butter

Prepare as for Buttered Flaked Almonds, but use bought garlic butter. This makes a smart topping for dishes like mashed potato and can also be added to creamy soups.

Dried Chestnuts

The microwave enables dried chestnuts to be cooked and usable in under 2 hours without soaking overnight followed by prolonged cooking. Also the hard job of peeling has already been done for you.

Wash 250 g/8 oz/2 cups dried chestnuts. Put into a 1.75 litre/3 pt/7½ cup dish. Stir in 600 ml/1 pt/2½ cups boiling water. Cover with a plate and cook on Full for 15 minutes, turning the dish three times. Stand in the microwave for 15 minutes. Repeat with the same cooking and standing times. Uncover, add a further 150 ml/¼ pt/2/3 cup boiling water and stir round. Cover as before and cook on Full for 10 minutes, stirring twice. Allow to stand for 15 minutes before using.

Drying Herbs

If you grow your own herbs but find it difficult to dry them in a damp and unpredictable climate, the microwave will do the job for you effectively, efficiently and cleanly in next to no time, so your annual crop can be savoured through the winter months. Each variety of herb should be dried by itself to keep the flavour intact. If you want to later on, you can make up your own blends by mixing several dried herbs together.

Start by cutting the herbs off their shrubs with secateurs or scissors. Pull the leaves (needles in the case of rosemary) off the stalks and pack them loosely into a 300 ml/½ pt/1¼ cup measuring jug, filling it almost to overflowing. Tip into a colander (strainer) and rinse them quickly and gently under cold running water. Drain thoroughly, then dry between the folds of a clean, dry tea towel (dish cloth). Put on top of a double thickness of kitchen paper placed directly on the microwave turntable. Heat, uncovered, on Full for 5–6 minutes, carefully moving the herbs about on the paper two or three times. As soon as they sound like autumn leaves rustling and have lost their bright green colour, you can assume the herbs are dried through. If not, continue to heat for 1–1½ minutes. Remove from the oven and allow to cool. Crush the dried herbs by rubbing them between your hands.

Transfer to airtight jars with stoppers and label. Store away from bright light.

Crisping Breadcrumbs

High-quality pale breadcrumbs – as opposed to marigold-yellow packet ones – are made perfectly in the microwave and turn crisp and brittle without browning. The bread can be fresh or stale but fresh will take a little longer to dry. Crumble 3½ large slices of white or brown bread with crusts into fine crumbs. Spread the crumbs into a shallow 25 cm/10 in diameter dish. Cook, uncovered, on Full for 5–6 minutes, stirring four times, until you can feel in your fingers that the crumbs are dry and crisp. Allow to cool, stirring round from time to time, then store in an airtight container. They will keep almost indefinitely in a cool place.

Nut Burgers

Makes 12

These are by no means new, particularly to vegetarians and vegans, but the combination of nuts gives these burgers an outstanding flavour, and the crunchy texture is equally appetising. They can be served hot with a sauce, cold with salad and mayonnaise, halved horizontally and used as a sandwich filling, or eaten just as they are for a snack.

30 ml/2 tbsp butter or margarine
125 g/4 oz/1 cup unskinned whole almonds
125 g/4 oz/1 cup pecan nut pieces
125 g/4 oz/1 cup cashew nut pieces, toasted
125 g/4 oz/2 cups fresh soft brown breadcrumbs
1 medium onion, grated
2.5 ml/½ tsp salt
5 ml/1 tsp made mustard
30 ml/2 tbsp cold milk

Melt the butter or margarine, uncovered, on Full for 1–1½ minutes. Grind the nuts fairly finely in a blender or food processor. Tip out and combine with the remaining ingredients including the butter or margarine. Divide into 12 equal pieces and shape into ovals. Arrange round the edge of a large greased plate. Cook, uncovered, on Full for 4 minutes, turning once. Allow to stand for 2 minutes.

Nutkin Cake

Serves 6–8

Prepare as for Nut Burgers, but substitute 350 g/12 oz/3 cups ground mixed nuts of your choice for the almonds, pecans and cashews. Shape into a 20 cm/8 in round and put on a greased plate. Cook, uncovered, on Full for 3 minutes. Allow to stand for 5 minutes, then cook on Full for a further 2½ minutes. Allow to stand for 2 minutes. Serve hot or cold, cut into wedges.

Buckwheat

Serves 4

Also known as Saracen corn and native to Russia, buckwheat is related to no other grain. It is the small fruit of a sweetly perfumed pink-flowering plant which is a member of the dock family. The basis of blinis (or Russian pancakes), the grain is a hearty, earthy staple and is a healthy substitute for potatoes with meat and poultry.

175 g/6 oz/1 cup buckwheat
1 egg, beaten
5 ml/1 tsp salt
750 ml/1¼ pts/3 cups boiling water

Mix the buckwheat and egg in a 2 litre/3½ pt/8½ cup dish. Toast, uncovered, on Full for 4 minutes, stirring and breaking up with a fork every minute. Add the salt and water. Stand on a plate in the microwave in case of spillage and cook, uncovered, on Full for 22 minutes, stirring four times. Cover with a plate and allow to stand for 4 minutes. Fork round before serving.

Bulgar

Serves 6–8

Also called burghal, burghul or cracked wheat, this grain is one of the staples of the Middle East. It is now widely available from supermarkets and health food shops.

225 g/8 oz/1¼ cups bulgar
600 ml/1 pt/2½ cups boiling water
5–7.5 ml/1–1½ tsp salt

Put the bulgar in a 1.75 litre/3 pt/7½ cup dish. Toast, uncovered, on Full for 3 minutes, stirring every minute. Stir in the boiling water and salt. Cover with a plate and allow to stand for 6–15 minutes, depending on the variety of bulgar used, until the grain is al dente, like pasta. Fluff up with a fork and eat hot or cold.

Bulgar with Fried Onion

Serves 4

1 onion, grated
15 ml/1 tbsp olive or sunflower
1 quantity Bulgar

Put the onion and oil in a small dish. Cook, uncovered, on Full for 4 minutes, stirring three times. Add to the cooked bulgar at the same time as the water and salt.

Tabbouleh

Serves 4

Coloured deep green by the parsley, this dish evokes the Lebanon and is one of the most appetising salads imaginable, a perfect accompaniment to many dishes from vegetarian nut cutlets to roast lamb. It also makes an attractive starter, arranged over salad greens on individual plates.

1 quantity Bulgar
120–150 ml/4–5 fl oz/½–2/3 cup finely chopped flatleaf parsley
30 ml/2 tbsp chopped mint leaves
1 medium onion, finely grated
15 ml/1 tbsp olive oil
Salt and freshly ground black pepper
Salad leaves
Diced tomatoes, diced cucumber and black olives, to garnish

Cook the bulgar as directed. Transfer half the quantity to a bowl and mix in the parsley, mint, onion, oil and plenty of salt and pepper to taste. When cold, arrange on salad leaves and decorate attractively with the garnish. Use the remaining bulgar in any way you wish.

Sultan's Salad

Serves 4

A personal favourite and, topped with pieces of Feta cheese and served with pitta bread, it makes a complete meal.

1 quantity Bulgar
1–2 garlic cloves, crushed
1 carrot, grated
15 ml/1 tbsp chopped mint leaves
60 ml/4 tbsp chopped parsley
Juice of 1 large lemon, strained
45 ml/3 tbsp olive or sunflower oil, or a mixture of both
Salad greens
Toasted almonds and green olives, to garnish

Cook the bulgar as directed, then stir in the garlic, carrot, mint, parsley, lemon juice and oil. Arrange on a plate lined with salad greens and stud with toasted almonds and green olives.

Couscous

Serves 4

Couscous is both a grain and the name of a North African meat or vegetable stew. Made from durum wheat semolina (cream of wheat), it looks like tiny, perfectly rounded pearls. It used to be hand-made by dedicated and talented home cooks but is now available in packets and can be cooked in a flash, thanks to a French technique that does away with the laborious and slow task of steaming. You can substitute couscous for any of the dishes made with bulgar (pages 209–10).

250 g/9 oz/1½ cups bought couscous
300 ml/½ pt/1¼ cups boiling water
5–10 ml/1–2 tsp salt

Put the couscous in a 1.75 litre/3 pt/7½ cup dish and toast, uncovered, on Full for 3 minutes, stirring every minute. Add the water and salt and fork round. Cover with a plate and cook on Full for 1 minute. Allow to stand in the microwave for 5 minutes. Fluff up with a fork before serving.

Grits

Serves 4

Grits (hominy grits) is a an almost-white North American cereal based on maize (corn). It is eaten with hot milk and sugar or with butter and salt and pepper. It is available from speciality food shops like Harrods in London.

150 g/5 oz/scant 1 cup grits
150 ml/¼ pt/2/3 cup cold water
600 ml/1 pt/2½ cups boiling water
5 ml/1 tsp salt

Put the grits in a 2.5 litre/4½ pt/11 cup bowl. Mix smoothly with the cold water, then stir in the boiling water and salt. Cook, uncovered, on Full for 8 minutes, stirring four times. Cover with a plate and allow to stand for 3 minutes before serving.

Gnocchi alla Romana

Serves 4

Gnocchi is often to be found in Italian restaurants, where it is well liked. It makes a substantial and wholesome lunch or supper dish with salad and uses economical ingredients.

600 ml/1 pt/2½ cups cold milk
150 g/5 oz/¾ cup semolina (cream of wheat)
5 ml/1 tsp salt
50 g/2 oz/¼ cup butter or margarine
75 g/3 oz/¾ cup grated Parmesan cheese
2.5 ml/½ tsp continental made mustard
1.5 ml/¼ tsp grated nutmeg
1 large egg, beaten
Mixed salad
Tomato ketchup (catsup)

Mix half the cold milk smoothly with the semolina in a 1.5 litre/2½ pt/6 cup dish. Heat the remaining milk, uncovered, on Full for 3 minutes. Stir into the semolina with the salt. Cook, uncovered, on Full for 7 minutes until very thick, stirring four or five times to keep the mixture smooth. Remove from the microwave and mix in half the butter, half the cheese and all the mustard, nutmeg and egg. Cook, uncovered, on Full for 1 minute. Cover with a plate and allow to stand for 1 minute. Spread in an oiled or buttered shallow 23 cm/9 in square dish. Cover loosely with kitchen paper and leave in the cool until firm and set. Cut into 2.5 cm/1 in squares. Arrange in a 23 cm/9 in buttered round dish in overlapping rings. Sprinkle with the remaining cheese, dot with flakes of the remaining butter and reheat in a hot oven for 15 minutes until golden brown. Serve very hot with salad and tomato sauce.

Ham Gnocchi

Serves 4

Prepare as for Gnocchi alla Romana, but add 75 g/3 oz/¾ cup chopped Parma ham with the warm milk.

Millet

Serves 4–6

A pleasing and delicate grain, related to sorghum, which is an off-beat substitute for rice. If eaten with pulses (peas, beans and lentils), it makes a well-balanced, protein-rich meal.

175 g/6 oz/1 cup millet
750 ml/1¼ pts/3 cups boiling water or stock
5 ml/1 tsp salt

Put the millet in a 2 litre/3½ pt/8½ cup dish. Toast, uncovered, on Full for 4 minutes, stirring twice. Mix in the water and salt. Stand on a plate in case of spillage. Cook, uncovered, on Full for 20–25 minutes until all the water has been absorbed. Fluff up with a fork and eat straight away.

Polenta

Serves 6

A bright yellow grain made from corn, similar to semolina (cream of wheat) but coarser. It is a staple starch food in Italy and Romania, where it is much respected and often eaten as a side dish with meat, poultry, egg and vegetable dishes. In recent years it has become a trendy restaurant speciality, often cut into squares and served grilled (broiled) or fried (sautéed) with the sauces similar to those used for spaghetti.

150 g/5 oz/¾ cup polenta
5 ml/1 tsp salt
125 ml/¼ pt/2/3 cup cold water
600 ml/1 pt/2½ cups boiling water or stock

Put the polenta and salt in a 2 litre/3½ pt/8½ cup dish. Blend smoothly with the cold water. Gradually mix in the boiling water or stock. Stand on a plate in case of spillage. Cook, uncovered, on Full for 7–8 minutes until very thick, stirring four times. Cover with a plate and allow to stand for 3 minutes before serving.

Grilled Polenta

Serves 6

Prepare as for Polenta. When cooked, spread in a buttered or oiled 23 cm/9 in square dish. Smooth the top with a knife dipped in and out of hot water. Cover loosely with kitchen paper and allow to cool completely. Cut into squares, brush with olive or corn oil and grill (broil) or fry (sauté) conventionally until golden brown.

Polenta with Pesto

Serves 6

Prepare as for Polenta, but add 20 ml/4 tsp red or green pesto with the boiling water.

Polenta with Sun-dried Tomato or Olive Paste

Serves 6

Prepare as for Polenta, but add 45 ml/3 tbsp sun-dried tomato or olive paste with the boiling water.

Quinoa

Serves 2–3

A fairly new-on-the-scene high-protein grain from Peru with a curiously crunchy texture and slightly smoky flavour. It goes with all foods and makes a novel substitute for rice.

125 g/4 oz/2/3 cup quinoa
2.5 ml/½ tsp salt
550 ml/18 fl oz/2 1/3 cups boiling water

Put the quinoa in a 1.75 litre/3 pt/7½ cup bowl. Toast, uncovered, on Full for 3 minutes, stirring once. Add the salt and water and mix in thoroughly. Cook on Full for 15 minutes, stirring four times. Cover and allow to stand for 2 minutes.

Romanian Polenta

Serves 4

Romania's notoriously rich national dish – mamaliga.

1 quantity Polenta
75 g/3 oz/1/3 cup butter
4 freshly poached large eggs
100 g/4 oz/1 cup Feta cheese, crumbled
150 ml/¼ pt/2/3 cup soured (dairy sour) cream

Prepare the polenta and leave in the dish in which it was cooked. Beat in half the butter. Spoon equal mounds on to four warmed plates and make an indentation in each. Fill with the eggs, sprinkle with the cheese and top with the remaining butter and the cream. Eat straight away.

Curried Rice

Serves 4

Suitable as an accompaniment for most oriental and Asiatic foods, especially Indian.

30 ml/2 tbsp groundnut (peanut) oil
2 onions, finely chopped
225 g/8 oz/1 cup basmati rice
2 small bay leaves
2 whole cloves
Seeds from 4 cardamom pods
30–45 ml/2–3 tbsp mild curry powder
5 ml/1 tsp salt
600 ml/1 pt/2½ cups boiling water or vegetable stock

Put the oil in a 2.25 litre/4 pt/10 cup dish. Heat, uncovered, on Full for 1 minute. Mix in the onions. Cook, uncovered, on Full for 5 minutes. Stir in all the remaining ingredients. Cover with clingfilm (plastic wrap) and slit it twice to allow steam to escape. Cook on Full for 15 minutes, turning the dish four times. Allow to stand for 2 minutes. Fork round lightly and serve.

Cottage Cheese and Rice Casserole

Serves 3–4

A great amalgam of tastes and textures brought back from North America some years ago.

225 g/8 oz/1 cup brown rice
50 g/2 oz/¼ cup wild rice
1.25 litre/2¼ pts/5½ cups boiling water
10 ml/2 tsp salt
4 spring onions (scallions), coarsely chopped
1 small green chilli, seeded and chopped
4 tomatoes, blanched, skinned and sliced
125 g/4 oz button mushrooms, sliced
225 g/8 oz/1 cup cottage cheese
75 g/3 oz/¾ cup Cheddar cheese, grated

Put the brown and wild rice in a 2.25 litre/4 pt/10 cup dish. Stir in the water and salt. Cover with clingfilm (plastic wrap) and slit it twice to allow steam to escape. Cook on Full for 40–45 minutes until the rice is plump and tender. Drain, if necessary, and set aside. Fill a 1.75 litre/3 pt/7½ cup casserole dish (Dutch oven) with alternate layers of rice, onions, chilli, tomatoes, mushrooms and cottage cheese. Sprinkle thickly with the grated Cheddar. Cook, uncovered, on Full for 7 minutes, turning the dish twice.

Italian Risotto

Serves 2–3

2.5–5 ml/½–1 tsp saffron powder or 5 ml/1 tsp saffron strands
50 g/2 oz/¼ cup butter
5 ml/1 tsp olive oil
1 large onion, peeled and grated
225 g/8 oz/1 cup easy-cook risotto rice
600 ml/1 pt/2½ cups boiling water or chicken stock
150 ml/¼ pt/2/3 cup dry white wine
5 ml/1 tsp salt
50 g/2 oz/½ cup grated Parmesan cheese

If using saffron strands, crumble them between your fingers into an egg cup of hot water and allow to stand for 10–15 minutes. Put half the butter and the oil in a 1.75 litre/3 pt/7½ cup dish. Heat, uncovered, on Defrost for 1 minute. Stir in the onion. Cook, uncovered, on Full for 5 minutes. Stir in the rice, water or stock and wine and either the saffron strands with the water, or the saffron powder. Cover with clingfilm (plastic wrap) and slit it twice to allow steam to escape. Cook on Full for 14 minutes, turning the dish three times. Gently fork in the remaining butter, followed by the salt and half the Parmesan cheese. Cook, uncovered, on Full for 4–8 minutes, stirring gently with a fork every 2 minutes, until the rice has absorbed all the liquid. The cooking time will depend on the rice used. Spoon into dishes and sprinkle the remaining cheese on top.

Mushroom Risotto

Serves 2–3

Break 20 g/1 oz dried mushrooms, porcini for preference, into smallish pieces, wash thoroughly under cold running water and then soak them for 10 minutes in the boiling water or chicken stock used in the Italian Risotto recipe. Proceed as for Italian Risotto.

Brazilian Rice

Serves 3–4

15 ml/1 tbsp olive or corn oil
30 ml/2 tbsp dried onion
225 g/8 oz/1 cup American long-grain or basmati rice
5–10 ml/1–2 tsp salt
600 ml/1 pt/2½ cups boiling water
2 large tomatoes, blanched, skinned and chopped

Pour the oil in a 2 litre/3½ pt/8½ cup dish. Add the dried onion. Cook, uncovered, on Full for 1¼ minutes. Stir in all the remaining ingredients. Cover with clingfilm (plastic wrap) and slit it twice to allow steam to escape. Cook on Full for 15 minutes, turning the dish four times. Allow to stand for 2 minutes. Fork round lightly and serve.

Spanish Rice

Serves 6

A North American special that has little to do with Spain other than the addition of peppers and tomatoes! Eat with poultry and egg dishes.

225 g/8 oz/1 cup easy-cook long-grain rice
600 ml/1 pt/2½ cups boiling water
10 ml/2 tsp salt
30 ml/2 tbsp corn or sunflower oil
2 onions, finely chopped
1 green (bell) pepper, seeded and coarsely chopped
400 g/14 oz/1 large can chopped tomatoes

Cook the rice in the water with half the salt as directed. Keep hot. Pour the oil into a 1.75 litre/3 pt/7½ cup bowl. Heat, uncovered, on Full for 1 minute. Stir in the onions and pepper. Cook, uncovered, on Full for 5 minutes, stirring twice. Mix in the tomatoes. Heat, uncovered, on Full for 3½ minutes. Fork in the hot rice with the remaining salt and serve straight away.

Plain Turkish Pilaf

Serves 4

225 g/8 oz/1 cup easy-cook risotto rice
Boiling water or vegetable stock
5 ml/1 tsp salt
40 g/1½ oz/3 tbsp butter

Cook the rice in the boiling water or stock with the salt added as directed. Add the butter to the dish or bowl. Allow to stand for 10 minutes. Uncover and fork round. Cover with a plate and reheat on Full for 3 minutes.

Rich Turkish Pilaf

Serves 4

225 g/8 oz/1 cup easy-cook risotto rice
Boiling water
5 ml/1 tsp salt
5 cm/2 in piece cinnamon stick
40 g/1½ oz/3 tbsp butter
15 ml/1 tbsp olive oil
2 onions, finely chopped
60 ml/4 tbsp toasted pine nuts
25 g/1 oz lambs' or chicken liver, cut into small pieces
30 ml/2 tbsp currants or raisins
2 tomatoes, blanched, skinned and chopped

Cook the rice in the water and salt, in a large dish or bowl, as directed with the cinnamon stick added. Set aside. Put the butter and oil in a 1.25 litre/2¼ pt/5½ cup bowl and heat, uncovered, on Full for 1 minute. Mix in all the remaining ingredients. Cover with a plate and cook on Full for 5 minutes, stirring twice. Stir gently into the hot rice with a fork. Cover as before and reheat on Full for 2 minutes.

Thai Rice with Lemon Grass, Lime Leaves and Coconut

Serves 4

A marvel of exquisite delicacy, appropriate for all Thai-style chicken and fish dishes.

250 g/9 oz/generous 1 cup Thai rice
400 ml/14 fl oz/1¾ cups canned coconut milk
2 fresh lime leaves
1 blade lemon grass, split lengthways, or 15 ml/1 tbsp chopped lemon balm leaves
7.5 ml/1½ tsp salt

Tip the rice into a 1.5 litre/2½ pt/6 cup dish. Pour the coconut milk into a measuring jug and make up to 600 ml/1 pt/2½ cups with cold water. Heat, uncovered, on Full for 7 minutes until it begins to bubble and boil. Stir gently into the rice with all the remaining ingredients. Cover with clingfilm (plastic wrap) and slit it twice to allow steam to escape. Cook on Full for 14 minutes. Allow to stand for 5 minutes. Uncover and remove the lemon grass, if used. Fork round gently and eat the slightly soft and sticky rice straight away.

Okra with Cabbage

Serves 6

A curiosity from the Gabon, mild or hot depending on the amount of chilli included.

30 ml/2 tbsp groundnut (peanut) oil
450 g/1 lb Savoy cabbage or spring greens (collard greens), finely shredded
200 g/7 oz okra (ladies' fingers), topped, tailed and cut into chunks
1 onion, grated
300 ml/½ pt/1¼ cups boiling water
10 ml/2 tsp salt
45 ml/3 tbsp pine nuts, lightly toasted under the grill (broiler)
2.5–20 ml/¼–4 tsp chilli powder

Pour the oil into a 2.25 litre/4 pt/10 cup casserole dish (Dutch oven). Stir in the greens and okra followed by the remaining ingredients. Mix well. Cover with clingfilm (plastic wrap) and slit it twice to allow steam to escape. Cook on Full for 7 minutes. Allow to stand for for 5 minutes. Cook on Full for a further 3 minutes. Drain if necessary and serve.

Red Cabbage with Apple

Serves 8

Magnificent with hot gammon, goose and duck, red cabbage is of Scandinavian and North European descent, a sweet-sour and now quite smart side dish, on its best behaviour in the microwave where it stays a deep rosy colour.

900 g/2 lb red cabbage
450 ml/¾ pt/2 cups boiling water
7.5 ml/1½ tsp salt
3 onions, finely chopped
3 cooking (tart) apples, peeled and grated
30 ml/2 tbsp light soft brown sugar
2.5 ml/½ tsp caraway seeds
30 ml/2 tbsp cornflour (cornstarch)
45 ml/3 tbsp malt vinegar
15 ml/1 tbsp cold water

Trim the cabbage, removing any bruised or damaged outer leaves. Cut into quarters and remove the hard central stalk, then shred as finely as possible. Put into a 2.25 litre/4 pt/10 cup dish. Add half the boiling water and 5 ml/1 tsp of the salt. Cover with a plate and cook on Full for 10 minutes, turning the dish four times. Stir well, then mix in the remaining boiling water and remaining salt, the onions, apples, sugar and caraway seeds. Cover with clingfilm (plastic wrap) and slit it twice to allow steam to escape. Cook on Full for 20 minutes, turning the dish four times. Remove from the microwave. Mix the cornflour smoothly with the vinegar and cold water. Add to the hot cabbage and mix well. Cook, uncovered, on Full for 10 minutes, stirring three times. Leave until cold before chilling overnight. To serve, re-cover with fresh clingfilm and slit it twice to allow steam to escape, then heat on Full for 5–6 minutes before serving. Alternatively, transfer portions to side plates and cover each with kitchen paper, then reheat individually on Full for 1 minute each.

Red Cabbage with Wine

Serves 8

Prepare as for Red Cabbage with Apples, but substitute 250 ml/8 fl oz/1 cup red wine for half the boiling water.

Norwegian Sour Cabbage

Serves 8

900 g/2 lb white cabbage
90 ml/6 tbsp water
60 ml/4 tbsp malt vinegar
60 ml/4 tbsp granulated sugar
10 ml/2 tsp caraway seeds
7.5–10 ml/1½–2 tsp salt

Trim the cabbage, removing any bruised or damaged outer leaves. Cut into quarters and remove the hard central stalk, then shred as finely as possible. Put into a 2.25 litre/4 pt/10 cup dish with all the remaining ingredients. Mix thoroughly with two spoons. Cover with clingfilm (plastic wrap) and slit it twice to allow steam to escape. Cook on Defrost for 45 minutes, turning the dish four times. Leave at kitchen temperature overnight for the flavours to mature. To serve, put individual servings on to side plates and cover each with kitchen paper. Reheat individually on Full, allowing about 1 minute each. Securely cover and then refrigerate any leftovers.

Greek-style Stewed Okra with Tomatoes

Serves 6–8

Very marginally Eastern in character, this slightly off-beat vegetable dish has become a viable proposition now that okra (ladies' fingers) is more widely available. This recipe is excellent with lamb or as a dish in its own right, served with rice.

900 g/2 lb okra, topped and tailed
Salt and freshly ground black pepper
90 ml/6 tbsp malt vinegar
45 ml/3 tbsp olive oil
2 onions, peeled and finely chopped
6 tomatoes, blanched, skinned and coarsely chopped
15 ml/1 tbsp light soft brown sugar

Spread out the okra on a large flat plate. To reduce the chances of the okra splitting and taking on a slimy feel, sprinkle with salt and the vinegar. Allow to stand for for 30 minutes. Wash and wipe dry on kitchen paper. Pour the oil into a 2.5 litre/4½ pt/11 cup dish and add the onions. Cook, uncovered, on Full for 7 minutes, stirring three times. Stir in all the remaining ingredients including the okra and season to taste. Cover with a plate and cook on Full for 9–10 minutes, stirring three or four times, until the okra is tender. Allow to stand for 3 minutes before serving.

Greens with Tomatoes, Onions and Peanut Butter

Serves 4–6

Try this Malawi speciality with sliced white bread as a vegetarian main course or serve as a side dish with chicken.

450 g/1 lb spring greens (collard greens), finely shredded
150 ml/¼ pt/2/3 cup boiling water
5–7.5 ml/1–1½ tsp salt
4 tomatoes, blanched, skinned and sliced
1 large onion, finely chopped
60 ml/4 tbsp crunchy peanut butter

Place the greens in a 2.25 litre/4 pt/10 cup dish. Mix in the water and salt. Cover with clingfilm (plastic wrap) and slit it twice to allow steam to escape. Cook on Full for 20 minutes. Uncover and stir in the tomatoes, onion and peanut butter. Cover as before and cook on Full for 5 minutes.

Sweet-sour Creamed Beetroot

Serves 4

This attractive way of presenting beetroot dates back to 1890, but it's currently back in fashion.

450 g/1 lb cooked beetroot (red beets), coarsely grated
150 ml/¼ pt/2/3 cup double (heavy) cream
Salt
15 ml/1 tbsp vinegar
30 ml/2 tbsp demerara sugar

Put the beetroot in a 900 ml/1½ pt/3¾ cup dish with the cream and salt to taste. Cover with a plate and heat through on Full for 3 minutes, stirring once. Stir in the vinegar and sugar and serve straight away.

Beetroot in Orange

Serves 4–6

A lively and original accompaniment to Christmas meats and poultry.

450 g/1 lb cooked beetroot (red beets), peeled and sliced
75 ml/5 tbsp freshly squeezed orange juice
15 ml/1 tbsp malt vinegar
2.5 ml/½ tsp salt
1 garlic clove, peeled and crushed

Place the beetroot in a shallow 18 cm/7 in diameter dish. Beat together the remaining ingredients and pour over the beetroot. Cover with clingfilm (plastic wrap) and slit it twice to allow steam to escape. Cook on Full for 6 minutes, turning the dish three times. Allow to stand for 1 minute.

Scalloped Celeriac

Serves 6

A handsome and gourmet-style winter side dish that teams happily with fish and poultry.

4 lean rashers (slices) bacon, chopped
900 g/2 lb celeriac (celery root)
300 ml/½ pt/1¼ cups cold water
15 ml/1 tbsp lemon juice
7.5 ml/1½ tsp salt
300 ml/½ pt/1¼ cups single (light) cream
1 small bag potato crisps (chips), crushed in the bag

Put the bacon on a plate and cover with kitchen paper. Cook on Full for 3 minutes. Peel the celeriac thickly, wash well and cut each head into eight pieces. Place in a 2.25 litre/4 pt/10 cup dish with the water, lemon juice and salt. Cover with clingfilm (plastic wrap) and slit it twice to allow steam to escape. Cook on Full for 20 minutes, turning the dish four times. Drain. Slice the celeriac and return to the dish. Stir in the bacon and cream and sprinkle with the crisps. Cook, uncovered, on Full for 4 minutes, turning the dish twice. Allow to stand for 5 minutes before serving.

Celeriac with Orange Hollandaise Sauce

Serves 6

Celeriac with a gloriously golden, gleaming topping of citrus Hollandaise sauce to try with duck and game.

900 g/2 lb celeriac (celery root)
300 ml/½ pt/1¼ cups cold water
15 ml/1 tbsp lemon juice
7.5 ml/1½ tsp salt
Maltese Sauce
1 very sweet orange, peeled and segmented

Peel the celeriac thickly, wash well and cut each head into eight pieces. Place in a 2.25 litre/4 pt/10 cup dish with the water, lemon juice and salt. Cover with clingfilm (plastic wrap) and slit it twice to allow steam to escape. Cook on Full for 20 minutes, turning the dish four times. Drain. Slice the celeriac and return to the dish. Keep hot. Make the Maltese Sauce and spoon over the celeriac. Garnish with the orange segments.

Slimmers' Vegetable Pot

Serves 2

Prepare as for Slimmer's Fish Pot but omit the fish. Add the diced flesh of 2 avocados to the cooked vegetables with the spices and herbs. Cover and reheat on Full for 1½ minutes.

Slimmers' Vegetable Pot with Eggs

Serves 2

Prepare as for Slimmer's Vegetable Pot, but sprinkle each portion with 1 chopped hard-boiled (hard-cooked) egg.

Ratatouille

Serves 6–8

An explosion of Mediterranean flavours and colours is part and parcel of this glorious vegetable pot-pourri. Hot, cold or warm – it seems to go with everything.

60 ml/4 tbsp olive oil
3 onions, peeled and coarsely chopped
1–3 garlic cloves, crushed
225 g/8 oz courgettes (zucchini), thinly sliced
350 g/12 oz/3 cups cubed aubergine (eggplant)
1 large red or green (bell) pepper, seeded and chopped
3 ripe tomatoes, skinned, blanched and chopped
30 ml/2 tbsp tomato purée (paste)
20 ml/4 tsp light soft brown sugar
10 ml/2 tsp salt
45–60 ml/3–4 tbsp chopped parsley

Pour the oil into a 2.5 litre/4½ pt/11 cup dish. Heat, uncovered, on Full for 1 minute. Mix in the onions and garlic. Cook, uncovered, on Full for 4 minutes. Stir in all the remaining ingredients except half the parsley. Cover with a plate and cook on Full for 20 minutes, stirring three or four times. Uncover and cook on Full for 8–10 minutes, stirring four times, until most of the liquid has evaporated. Mix in the remaining parsley. Serve straight away or cool, cover and chill if to be eaten later.

Caramelised Parsnips

Serves 4

Ideal with all poultry and beef roasts, choose baby parsnips no bigger than large carrots for this.

450 g/1 lb small parsnips, thinly sliced
45 ml/3 tbsp water
25 g/1 oz/2 tbsp butter
7.5 ml/1½ tbsp dark soft brown sugar
Salt

Put the parsnips in a 1.25 litre/2¼ pt/5½ cup dish with the water. Cover with clingfilm (plastic wrap) and slit it twice to allow steam to escape. Cook on Full for 8–10 minutes, turning the dish and gently shaking the contents twice, until tender. Drain off the water. Add the butter and sugar and toss the parsnips to coat them thoroughly. Heat, uncovered, on Full for 1–1½ minutes until glazed. Sprinkle with salt and eat straight away.

Parsnips with Egg and Butter Crumb Sauce

Serves 4

450 g/1 lb parsnips, diced
45 ml/3 tbsp water
75 g/3 oz/1/3 cup unsalted (sweet) butter
4 spring onions (scallions), finely chopped
45 ml/3 tbsp light-coloured toasted breadcrumbs
1 hard-boiled (hard-cooked) egg, grated
30 ml/2 tbsp finely chopped parsley
Juice of ½ small lemon

Place the parsnips in a 1.5 litre/2½ pt/6 cup dish with the water. Cover with clingfilm (plastic wrap) and slit it twice to allow steam to escape. Cook on Full for 8–10 minutes. Allow to stand while preparing the sauce. Put the butter in a measuring jug and melt, uncovered, on Defrost for 2–2½ minutes. Stir in the onions and cook, uncovered, on Defrost for 3 minutes, stirring twice. Mix in all the remaining ingredients and heat on Defrost for 30 seconds. Drain the parsnips and transfer to a warmed serving dish. Coat with the crumb sauce and serve straight away.

Fonduta

Serves 4–6

An Italian version of Cheese Fondue, inordinately luscious.

Prepare as for Cheese Fondue, but substitute Italian Fontina cheese for the Gruyère (Swiss) and Emmental cheeses, dry white Italian wine for the Mosel, and marsala for the Kirsch.

Mock Cheese and Tomato Fondue

Serves 4–6

225 g/8 oz/2 cups mature Cheddar cheese, grated
125 g/4 oz/1 cup Lancashire or Wensleydale cheese, crumbled
300 ml/10 fl oz/1 can condensed tomato soup
10 ml/2 tsp Worcestershire sauce
A dash of hot pepper sauce
45 ml/3 tbsp dry sherry
Warmed ciabatta bread, to serve

Place all the ingredients except the sherry in a 1.25 litre/2¼ pt/5½ cup glass or pottery dish. Cook, uncovered, on Defrost for 7–9 minutes, stirring three or four times, until the fondue is smoothly thickened. Remove from the microwave and stir in the sherry. Eat with pieces of warm ciabatta bread.

Mock Cheese and Celery Fondue

Serves 4–6

Prepare as for Mock Cheese and Tomato Fondue, but substitute condensed celery soup for the tomato soup and flavour with gin instead of sherry.

Italian Cheese, Cream and Egg Fondue

Serves 4–6

1 garlic clove, crushed

50 g/2 oz/¼ cup unsalted (sweet) butter, at kitchen temperature

450 g/1 lb/4 cups Fontina cheese, grated

60 ml/4 tbsp cornflour (cornstarch)

300 ml/½ pt/1¼ cups milk

2.5 ml/½ tsp grated nutmeg

Salt and freshly ground black pepper

150 ml/¼ pt/2/3 cup whipping cream

2 eggs, beaten

Cubed Italian bread, to serve

Place the garlic, butter, cheese, cornflour, milk and nutmeg in a deep 2.5 litre/4½ pt/11 cup glass or pottery dish. Season to taste. Cook, uncovered, on Full for 7–9 minutes, stirring four times, until the fondue begins to bubble gently. Remove from the microwave and mix in the cream. Cook, uncovered, on Full for 1 minute. Remove from the microwave and gradually beat in the eggs. Serve with Italian bread for dipping.

Dutch Farmhouse Fondue

Serves 4–6

A soft and gentle fondue, mild enough for children.

1 garlic clove, crushed
15 ml/1 tbsp butter
450 g/1 lb/4 cups Gouda cheese, grated
15 ml/1 tbsp cornflour (cornstarch)
20 ml/4 tsp mustard powder
A pinch of grated nutmeg
300 ml/½ pt/1¼ cup full-cream milk
Salt and freshly ground black pepper
Cubed bread, to serve

Place all the ingredients in a deep 2.5 litre/4½ pt/11 cup glass or pottery dish, seasoning well to taste. Cook, uncovered, on Full for 7–9 minutes, stirring four times, until the fondue begins to bubble gently. Bring the dish to the table and eat by spearing a cube of bread on to a long fondue fork, swirling it round in the cheese mixture, then lifting it out.

Farmhouse Fondue with a Kick

Serves 4–6

Prepare as for Dutch Farmhouse Fondue, but stir in 30–45 ml/2–3 tbsp Genever (Dutch gin) after cooking.

www.ingramcontent.com/pod-product-compliance
Lightning Source LLC
Chambersburg PA
CBHW071818080526
44589CB00012B/839